Discretion, Justice, and Democracy:
A Public Policy Perspective

Discretion, Justice, and Democracy

A Public Policy Perspective

EDITED BY

CARL F. PINKELE AND **WILLIAM C. LOUTHAN**

THE IOWA STATE UNIVERSITY PRESS / AMES

Composed and printed by The Iowa State University Press, Ames, Iowa 50010

First edition, 1985

Library of Congress Cataloging in Publication Data
Main entry under title:

Discretion, justice, and democracy.

"Product of three panel sessions . . . beginning with the annual meeting of American Society for Public Administration (ASPA) in Phoenix, Arizona, in 1978, and extending through the ASPA meeting in San Francisco, California, to the 1982 Academy of Criminal Justice Sciences meeting in Louisville, Kentucky"—Pref.
Bibliography: p.
Includes index.
1. Criminal justice, Administration of—United States—Addresses, essays, lectures. 2. Judicial discretion—United States—Addresses, essays, lectures. 3. Prosecution—United States—Decision making—Addresses, essays, lectures. 4. Police discretion—United States—Addresses, essays, lectures. I. Pinkele, Carl F. II. Louthan, William C. III. American Society for Public Administration. IV. Academy of Criminal Justice Sciences.
KF223.A75D57 1985   364'.973   84-22509
ISBN 0-8138-0466-3

CONTENTS

PREFACE

THIS VOLUME initially came to life as the product of three panel sessions organized and chaired by Carl F. Pinkele. Beginning with the annual meeting of American Society for Public Administration (ASPA) in Phoenix, Arizona, in 1978, and extending through the ASPA meeting in San Francisco, California, to the 1982 Academy of Criminal Justice Sciences meeting in Louisville, Kentucky, papers were presented and discussed that focused on the role of discretion in the criminal justice process.

It is unusual that one relatively cohesive group should have had an opportunity for such a continuous and thorough examination of a topic. As editors we were able to take advantage of these three opportunities to refine and sharpen our collective focus.

For reasons of space and time it has not been possible to include all of the papers or authors and critics who participated at one stage or another in these panel sessions. To all who fit into these categories we express our appreciation for your contributions to this volume.

Special mention should be extended by the editors to the volume's contributors. It always takes time and a cooperative effort to put together any collection and this was no exception. The contributors were timely, patient, and receptive to any changes and delays that occurred.

Several persons have been central to the production of this book. It is important to note the vital role played by Janet King of the Ohio Wesleyan University Politics and Government Department. The staff and particularly Judith Gildner at Iowa State University Press have been skillful and friendly; they have orchestrated the various stages of production with exemplary professionalism.

Finally, it is important to mention the generally overwhelming support provided by our respective families. They endured our absences, suffered through our irritabilities when things did not flow smoothly, and were there to share in our excitement when things clicked; so to Barbara and Abigail Pinkele and Leslie, Lauren, and Mark Louthan — thank you.

INTRODUCTION

CARL F. PINKELE

THE PRESENCE of discretionary opportunities and behavior in the law implementation system is a significant public policy issue. One need hardly pay careful attention to find such matters as mandatory sentencing, harsher sentencing, and tighter restrictions for parole and bail on public and practitioners' agendas. These items directly and indirectly involve discretionary policymaking behavior, and they are issues about which there is considerable controversy and heated disagreement.

On several fronts there are positional and perceptual problems. If one refers to the existing volume of public opinion data, it seems an obvious conclusion that the public wants to restrict several discretionary opportunities or loopholes in the law implementation system. In a seemingly contradictory way, many of these same people would allow police more discretionary latitude and flexibility with arrest and postarrest powers. And it appears to be the case that the present majority on the Supreme Court share such "loosening" views.

The discretionary behavior issue is to be found in scholarly analyses as well. Perhaps the best known recent critic of a discretionary role in the law is Professor Kenneth Culp Davis. It is not easy to state briefly Professor Davis' theses or those of anyone else who has written about this intriguing topic. But Davis does appear to represent the main impressions of those who have addressed the existence of discretionary behavior—that is, discretion is held to be a generally unhealthy dimension of our law implementation system.

Not withstanding the strong views about its negative role in the law implementation system, discretionary judgments and policymaking continue to play crucial parts in the law drama. Two relative simple observations underscore the dictums that judicial discretion is an ever present element in the law implementation system and is a complex public policy issue. First, at every level and in each aspect of the system, as the essays in this volume demonstrate, authorities have opportunity to and *do* behave autonomously and exercise discretion. That is, persons situated in a position of authority basically decide how they will act toward those individuals under their supervision or within their decisional orbit. And, critically, the extent to which the respective authorities must consider the preferences and values of other actors in the system is to a large degree problematical. Second, the ability to act with relative autonomy and discretion is part of an institutional and systemic capacity that amply provides for such opportunities to exist. This volume focuses upon the complex questions presented by the inevitable and unavoidable presence of discretion within the law implementation system and the normative issues raised by its presence.

As with any attempt to render the world more comprehensible, so too does this volume require some clarification and specification of its terminology. Basically, *discretion* refers to the ability of one who occupies an official position in the law implementation system to act with considerable autonomy. When an individual or set of individuals has the capability of making decisions based upon personal choices or preferences without being behaviorally constrained in their actions by rules or by others in positions of greater authority, the resulting behavior is discretionary in nature.

Three important corollaries accompany this broad definition. First, the existence of autonomy is a relative as well as a comparative matter. One properly measures an actor's degree of discretion when he makes his choices. Dworkin is helpful here in suggesting that "discretion, like the hole in a doughnut, does not exist except as an area left open by a surrounding belt of restriction." This leads to the second corollary—that we must describe matters of the "hole": what rules govern or constrain behavior; who is to impose the constraints; and how are those constraints to be effected? Third, we must recognize that there are two basic modes of discretionary behavior: structural discretion and individual discretion.

Structural discretion obtains within an organizational framework when options are permissible according to a prefigurative established rule. Thus, for example, a general rule will allow for a range of possible behavior to put the rule into operation. In other words, there are a number of generally suitable and legitimate ways to "get to Rome." However, and this is most important, "getting to Rome" is the rule; its maximization is the guide by which behavior must be measured.

Individual discretion obtains when either one or both of two circumstances occur: (1) individuals in the law implementation system have no rule or policy guidelines by which to set their course and thus are able to act according to personal, rather than institutional or systemic, motives (a feature unlikely to occur in any organized environment, particularly one associated with the law process); or (2) individuals are able for one reason or another to chart a course independent of an existing rule, an existing set of policy guidelines, or superior rule interpreter. Because of the centrality of implementation within any political system, particularly one that professes to be democratic, the presence and impact of individual discretion is of upmost concern.

The *law implementation system* needs some preliminary explication. Briefly put, the law implementation system refers to those institutions charged with putting the country's laws into operation. In a technical sense authorities in the law implementation system do not make the law. They deliver, put into place, and carry out the laws made by those who are legitimately constituted to make them.

In a real sense, however, students and practitioners of public policy know that it is through the process of delivering or implementing policies that policies are actually made. This volume acknowledges the reality and the seriousness of the discretionary factor in public policy and probes the amount and the meaning of such behavior.

In Chapter 1 Carl F. Pinkele considers the complex normative question of how discretion squares with democratic theory. The central feature of this chapter is an examination of the traditional mainstream myth that in the cause of further-ing better government one should constrain discretionary policymaking, espe-cially across the law implementation system, through the development and appli-cation of more stringent rules. The author's contention, from a democratic theory perspective, is that on balance considerably more is to be gained by constraining discretionary practices within the framework of politics than by rule promulgation or implementation.

The long and complex history of how discretion has been both practiced and interpreted provides the focus for Chapter 2. William C. Louthan observes on the one hand that discretionary practices are ever present today, as they have been in the past, and there are benefits such as flexibility associated with it that are crucial to the successful operation of our law implementation system.

Beginning with Chapter 3, the focus turns from theoretical overviews to discussions of the rules and meanings of discretion throughout the several sepa-rate yet interconnected stages in the law implementation system. Chapters 3 to 8 reflect discretion's multifaceted presence across the spectrum from police behavior through the prison system.

In Chapter 3 Gregory H. Williams examines the issue of police discretionary behavior. He describes what is essentially an inverted pyramid of responsibility in which street officers exercise significant discretion in the arrest decision. Williams concludes that the police should be recognized as policymakers. Thus coordinated action should obtain when addressing this issue of police discretionary behavior.

Utilizing data from Hamilton County, Ohio, from April 1977 to March 1978, Fred Rhynhart in Chapter 4 analyzes judicial discretion at the practical release stage. Rhynhart finds that both structural and individual behavioral dis-cretion are extensive and bail-setting practices vary widely; furthermore, reform will be difficult in such a deeply ingrained zone of judicial autonomy.

Sidney I. Lezak and Maureen Leonard in Chapter 5 analyze prosecutorial discretion. They also find that the nature and scope of prosecutional discretion is rather wide and quite varied. Both environmental and structural factors clearly portend the continuation of a significant amount of prosecutor level discretion, and reforms must be initiated in an atmosphere that guarantees its continued existence.

Judicial behavior in so many ways is at the heart of the law implementation system. Consequently, judicial decisions reflect the structurally inherent discre-tionary nature of judicial sentencing behavior. In Chapter 6 Carl F. Pinkele ex-amines the extent of discretionary behavior by comparing the sentencing patterns of two New Orleans criminal court judges. Pinkele proposes that reforming the extensive discretionary orbit of judges begin by setting judicial behavior within a democratic political context.

Continuing the theme of the extensiveness of judicial discretion initiated by Pinkele in the previous chapter, in Chapter 7 David Kalinich examines discretion in sentencing and in the parole process. He finds that there is great disparity in the process that is not only related to what judges do but also to what information is provided them by probation authorities. Furthermore, Kalinich observes that attempts to restrict discretion have failed largely because of their formalistic character.

In Chapter 8 Jon M. Kinnamon discusses what he suggests has been the most autonomous and unrestricted arena of discretionary behavior—the administration of penal institutions. In this arena of generally unconstrained discretionary activity and opportunity, Kinnamon finds that efforts to achieve judicial review have been meaningful, although extensive possibilities remain for those in authority to proceed relatively unchecked by effective external constraints.

With this considerable popular and practitioner attention to discretionary behavior, what has been done at the federal level to check its continuation and expansion? According to Edward I. Sidlow and Beth H. Henschen in Chapter 9, the U.S. Congress has done very little to oversee the exercise of discretion. Discretionary decision making, according to the authors, is not attractive enough in its complexities to have warranted anything but piecemeal congressional attention. Thus if remedies for discretionary excesses are to be found, Sidlow and Henschen suggest that one begin with a realistic assessment of why in the real world of politics these issues are profoundly unattractive.

The last two chapters in the volume are concerned with different aspects of discretionary behavior involved in civil rights litigation and administration. In Chapter 10 Richard Salem discusses how Title X of the Civil Rights Act of 1964 and judicial discretion may enpower the Community Relations Service to act as an instrument for the mediation of civil rights cases. Mediation as an alternative to litigation, according to Salem, has offered judges an attractive course toward the resolution of complex social issues. Prior to its serious contraction because of post-1980 budget cuts, Salem finds the opportunities for judicially initiated discretionary mediation to be an exciting and useful alternative to the traditional attempts at resolving some civil rights matters.

Ball, Krane, and Lauth in Chapter 11 consider the extent and meaning of administrative discretion in Section 5 of the Voting Rights Act of 1965. Administrators of this act have frequently exercised discretion. These authors find that achieving the proper balance between the necessary policymaking flexibility and the required legislatively directed outcome is a difficult, delicate, and crucial one for practitioners and society.

After confronting the realities and the normative complexities of discretionary behavior analyzed in this volume, we believe that the reader—regardless of prior views—will be prepared for an informed response. Surely we have neither posed nor answered all of the questions and issues raised by discretion in the law implementation system. Our goals have been to stimulate discussion and elicit responses in the public market place of ideas. We suggest that these are appropriate in the effort to achieve better public policies in a democratic polity.

Discretion, Justice, and Democracy:
A Public Policy Perspective

CHAPTER ONE

Discretion Fits Democracy:
An Advocate's Argument

CARL F. PINKELE

THROUGHOUT the implementation of the law system, discretionary behavior is real and is frequently viewed as being anomalous for a democratic system.[1] Discretionary behavior has penetrated into each aspect of the law system; and yet according to several of our most potent symbols and myths such a reality should neither frequently occur nor be countenanced. The symbols and myths of the American political system reverberate with the implications of such expressions as "we are a nation of laws and not men." The thrust of such a nostrum is clearly contrary to the holding that public decisions, especially legal ones, should be the product of political or personal intentions.

The argument put forward here is not only that significant discretionary behavior does occur throughout the law implementation system but also, and more significantly, that much of it is potentially healthy for a democracy. Through first noticing and then critically evaluating the manner and results of discretionary behavior, three central features of concern for an indirect democracy can be measured: (1) the *accessibility* of public decision makers to those for whom they are acting, (2) the degree of *responsiveness* of public decision makers to requests for action, (3) the acceptance of *responsibility* and *accountability* for the making of what in fact are fiduciary decisions. I am by no means identifying these as the only important measures of democratic character. However, they are three keystones of a democratic system, and if they were not in place and operating it could well be impossible to make a rational case that a system is democratic.

Responsibility and accountability are perhaps most significant, for they relate directly to the necessary ability of the citizenry to assess the performance of its entrusted agents through such mechanisms as elections. At a minimum these three dimensions rest upon and attest to the fundamentally political aspects of decision making — they have, in other words, to do with who gets what, when, and how (which Harold Laswell has correctly instructed us to view as the heart and soul of politics.)

At first glance discretionary behavior may rub raw a democratic nerve because

Carl F. Pinkele, Ohio Wesleyan University, Delaware, Ohio.

of the hypothesized connection between discretion and tyranny. The trap seems usually to be sprung by something akin to Lord Acton's famous line that "power corrupts and absolute power corrupts absolutely." Thus, having any degree of power is to be viewed as inherently dangerous to others. Furthermore, to have power is to use it. The relationship between having power and employing power is imagined to be mechanical and axiomatic. The formal answer to the existence of individualized power is located in a set of institutional constraints. In the U.S. system these constraints are rules — the Constitution and lesser-level laws — and the division of powers and functions that arise from the checks and balances system.

Without the full and continual operation of the established constraints and the requisite vigilance of those charged with making them work properly, the prospects for democracy presumedly are endangered, because people with power can do more or less whatever they wish. As the constraints system is weakened, either by nonoperation or by circumvention, the threat of tyranny is seen to become real. When the focus is upon the discretion of public decision makers, the issue usually has been one of proposing more and tighter rules. It is in this light that Kenneth Culp Davis suggests "the desirability of administrative rules extends as far as discretionary power extends. Whenever any agency or officer has discretionary power, rule-making is appropriate."[2]

Generally speaking liberals are in accord with the position articulated by Davis (and in general it is the mainstream thought) in attempting to link the behavior of public decision makers to previously established rules. From this liberal perspective, the link is formal. The decision makers, according to liberal thought, should be allowed little other than the most minimal form of "weak discretion," as Ronald Dworkin uses that phrase. According to Dworkin's reading, "We use 'discretion' in a weak sense simply to say that for some reason the standards an official must apply cannot be applied mechanically but demand the use of judgment."[3] That is, within what can be called mainstream liberal thought, it is held that the more constraints in place to restrict discretionary administrative interpretation and implementation, the better off we are as a democratic people.

The position presented in this chapter, however, is that the weaker (more general), more broadly humanistic and pluralistic the lines tethering a decision maker, the better off we are potentially within a democratic polity. It is precisely through the fuller exercise of Dworkin's sense of weak discretion that our chances for enhancing and advancing democracy should occur.

Democracy is the quintessential political system. In a democracy the widest scope should be provided for citizens participating in the selection and evaluation of decision makers. Through allowing public officials to exercise judgment and enabling the citizenry to evaluate those judgements the purposes of democracy are advanced. Furthermore, the objectives of decision making — including especially those within the law system — are political, and the most important constraints upon them also should be political.

DISCRETION AND TYRANNY

The overwhelming historical and symbolic hurdle confronting the legitimation of discretionary behavior is that individual or particularistic behavior is associated with tyranny. Power (authority to act plus the will to act) has been and is associated, often correctly, with the ability to abuse one's position. Lord Acton's observation on the malignancy of power succinctly sums up the general liberal fear of government. It has been combined in American mythology with the historical circumstances of the tyranny of George III, the onset of the American Revolution, and the countervailing limitations upon power within government that were established by the Constitution.[4]

Tyranny has been viewed as the archenemy of democracy. A tyrannical government is one seen as unprincipled, capricious, and unpredictable, and is one in which decision makers make personally biased and generally self-serving decisions. Tyranny is held to be anathema to a liberal democracy in which the general tenets are a government predicated upon the Lincolnesque notions, "of, by, and for the people"; equity in treatment; fairness and justice; and, for liberals, the observance of law and legal behavior. Most liberal democrats particularly would immediately embrace Kenneth Culp Davis's provocative challenge in opening the discussion in *Discretionary Justice* that "where law ends, tyranny begins."

It is the laws, of which the Constitution is the most symbolically important both in spirit and in fact, that for liberals are the bulwarks standing guard against illegitimate usurpation of authority. Therefore, constraining public officials' discretionary behavior through law is perceived in the liberal mind to be at the very core of a search for a healthy and democratic polity.

The law-as-preventer-of-tyranny perspective presents us with a crucial paradox. One cannot hold that laws and the people who make, enforce, and interpret them are qualitatively distinct entities. Laws have a historical, a cultural, a socioeconomic-political, and often a specifically individual character to them. All too often, particularly when they function as symbols, laws become reified and begin to take on an almost independent existence. In people's minds this myth-making process distances laws from their origins and their essential political qualities.[5]

At even the most formal level of activity and in the most sanitized model possible, the entanglement of people and law must remain an ongoing, tension-laden process. With rare exceptions, few serious analysts would or reasonably *could* join unreservedly with President Reagan who, for example, when confronted with a national strike of air traffic controllers in the summer of 1981, posited that the law was very clear and he had "no choice" but to fire them.

At least two conditions obtain simultaneously to seriously challenge Reagan's pinched and self-serving understanding of how law operates as a series of guideposts for policy actions. There is normally more than one law or precedent that can be selected as the beacon (this is particularly the case prior to any court deliberations on a matter). Nonlegal policy and political perspectives are always at work fashioning one's perspective as to what selection is the more appropriate choice. Furthermore, the appropriate choice of a particular law, or reading of it, almost invariably will contain all manner of nonlaw variables and factors. No matter how much is done to explicitly or symbolically exclude political considerations and calculations from public policy decisions, it cannot (and should not) be accomplished. There is no such thing as a politically uncontaminated choice in the law arena. Indeed, the resort to law either as symbol or as a body of rules to inhibit or resolve public conflict is inherently a political act. Second, it might well be "illegal" for the air traffic control union to have resorted to a protest action, but that proscribed action in no way necessarily prescribes a specific reaction on the part of one charged with administering the law. Again, remedies significantly involve political choices.

It is significant also to note that President Reagan's actions in firing the air traffic controllers took on additional political baggage because in this specific instance he acted as judge, jury, and executioner. Across an array of policy process dimensions he opened himself up to a charge of resorting to a nakedly political use of the law. Perhaps "legally" he should not have done so, but surely by so doing he usurped authority through a preemptive political act.

A generally agreed-upon point in the U.S. system—a system built around an explicit division of functions—is that implementing authorities should not take it upon themselves to provide a remedy for a unilaterally perceived wrongful act. By so acting, President Reagan clearly exercised discretion in perhaps its worst and most objectionable sense by voiding the concepts of checks and balances and separation of powers. Deflecting attention away from the essentially political nature of his actions through a symbolic cover of law opens up for all to see one aspect of the problem in a reliance upon rules as an effective barrier to wrongful behavior.

Perhaps no example of discretionary behavior at the macrolevel more clearly demonstrates the overarching political dimension of the law implementation system than the variety of circumventions associated with implementing the policy preferences expressed in *Brown v. Board of Education* (1954). Desegregation historically has met with all manner and modes of avoidance. At this writing, the Reagan administration's "reinterpretation" of tax exemption for colleges that practice racial segregation provides a contemporary example of the dominance of politics over law. The entirety of the black civil rights struggle has illustrated in sharp relief indeed that the law as judicially rendered is quite different from the law as policies finally implemented. The black struggle in general clearly displays the political impregnation of legal action and judgments. One cannot point with pride from a democratic vantage point to the avoidances and evasions that continue to pass for "all deliberate speed." Most critically, from the standpoint of this argument, one cannot avoid taking full notice of the very considerable extent to which one law is countered by another law and is then combined with interpretations, policy considerations, and political feasibility judgments across the policy implementation system. The civil rights thrust demonstrates beyond any shadow of doubt that law is politics by another means.

Throughout the unsatisfactory and incomplete course of establishing the fullest measure of civil rights and citizenship for black Americans, courts have undone other courts. Policymakers often have moved in seemingly casual and contradictory fashion to each other and to the courts. The overall terrain of civil rights policy generally resembles a massive pinball game, with "the law" and policy directives careening around in seemingly random fashion.

The only feature of the policy process that does seem to function continually and that remains solidly in place is that of discretionary behavior: it abounds within and between levels and jurisdictions. Indeed, viewed at this macrolevel, it would seem not at all to be the case that the United States is a nation of laws guiding people, but rather that people unabashedly fashion laws and interpretations of laws to suit broadly political interests and preferences.[6]

The message contained in this pattern of civil rights policy results is clear enough. The dialectic between law and person is more often than not resolved in favor of the individual policy actor; and the matter of the prospect or extent to which tyranny can spring forth is not vitiated, or perhaps even dampened, by having just laws or good interpretations.

At the microlevel in the law administration system, discretionary behavior is the fundamental mode of operation. Discretion is commonly referred to here as "selective enforcement." A frequently encountered circumstance provides an illuminating example of such selectivity in operation. The present highway speed limit is 55 mph. An operator of a vehicle traveling at 60 mph passes a highway patrol officer. The operator of the vehicle is not stopped, even though the driver's excessive and illegitimate speed registers on the patrol officer's radar gun. Such a brief but common example underscores the ever present nature of discretionary policymaking and policy-implementing behavior: (1) the law was clearly violated, but (2) the public person, employing discretionary judgment, did not choose to enforce it.

What often happens in this selective enforcement scenario is that a policy decision is made at levels higher than the individual patrol officer to overlook speeding transgressions until they have exceeded the law by X mph; or a small number of patrol officers decides among themselves to not ticket below a certain excessive speed; or a traffic judge either implicitly or explicitly informs ticketing personnel to "not come into my court with violations unless they have gone at least 65 mph;" or the individual patrol person, for any one of a number of personal reasons, decides against stopping the speeder. The list of possible scenarios is long, but the common denominator is telling. Individual discretion interacts with law to produce policy that hardly resembles the sorts of things one formally is taught to expect where rules are present to "guide" the actions of public officers. Some might argue that what is needed is more rules or better enforcement of them; I think not.

It is quite beyond being merely trivial that individuals make interpretations of, from, and about the law. Different individuals read the law differently; different individuals view the law differently; different individuals implement the law differently. This is not to say that there is no common meaning within the law system. Rather, it is to underscore the point that the grand symbolic postulate that "we are a nation of laws and not men" cannot be a sufficient barrier to tyrannical behavior, although it is probably in a number of ways a helpful barrier.

Laws, along with those structures and processes associated with their implementation, are inadequate as an independent barrier against tyranny. Having a rule in no way satisfactorily portends whether and how the rule shall be applied. To be sure, the law does not necessarily spawn tyranny; indeed, a law system should and could be an asset in preventing tyrannical behavior. Dworkin suggests that discretion is analogous to the hole in a doughnut. This being the case (and I believe it is) the ring should be democratic in character and quality, and the interior of the arena of discretion — the doughnut hole — should be judged accordingly. It is in this context that the measures of accessibility, responsiveness, and responsibility are brought into full play. The point is to democratize the exercise of discretion within the law implementation system and to analyze it subject to democratic standards, rather than to propose the illusion of more rules as "solutions."

DISCRETION AND DEMOCRACY

Included in most discussions of democracy is the point that a special relationship exists therein between those in positions of public authority and those who are not. Whether one is discussing a more direct democracy or an indirect representative situation makes little difference. In this decision makers–citizens relationship the governors have a strong fiduciary relationship to the governed. Democracy rests upon two notions: that the authority for making political decisions is derived from the sovereignty of the citizenry, and that interests as reflected in policy decisions shall not supplant or countervail the broad and general interests of all the public. In this construction, democracy must contain a continual integral commitment to the primacy of public, as opposed to private or individual, interests.

Democracy as viewed from within a Lockean-liberal-democratic perspective, on the other hand, builds upon a series of postulates about human nature and society in which the separation of public and private spheres of life is critical.[7] The fundamental building block for the Lockean mind is a metaphysical individualism wherein everything originates from the physical and egoistic separateness of one from another. As the result of this inherent separateness, humans are viewed "naturally" as being nonsocial. According to the Lockean liberal, society is constructed through the mechanism of the social contract and is, therefore, in a significant manner artificial. The chain of exchanges between one individual and another, between individuals and society, and between society and government is linked by autonomous actors pursuing their own goals within the confines of the social contract. A keystone of this Lockean construction is that private interests are viewed as generally more important than public concerns or interests. This set of liberal propositions is nicely captured by Brian Berry, who says that "the [liberal] vision of society is made up of independent, autonomous units who cooperate only when the terms of cooperation are such as make it further the ends of each of the parties."[8] The inherent and to a crucial extent irreconcilable tensions between person and society are to be regulated by limiting governments' abilities to act and by preserving individual rights through rules.

Rules (laws) are a centerpiece for the liberal perspective. It is through establishing and administering correct rules properly that the separation and preservation of private concerns from as much public intrusion as possible is to be accomplished. While sometimes some rules are a problem within this perspective, other rules are always the answer. Thus, when it comes to discretionary behavior within the law system, the liberal axiomatically searches for the resolution to dilemmas and problems by trying to create better formal rules.

A resort to law and rules is an intrinsically important strategy for western liberalism. Such is the case because the dominant version of liberalism—the Lockean one—either attempts to denigrate the political world and the value choices and conflicts associated with it altogether, or it relegates politics to a less than significant position in its hierarchy of values.[9] In these antipolitical contexts a resort to law performs two services for the typical liberal mind: (1) law is held to be universal, therefore neutral and "above" conflict; and (2) law and formal rules, including administrative ones, become the perceived and indeed the sanctioned focal points of decision making and controversy. In such a construction as this liberal one, what in large part occurs is that law symbolically displaces politics and fuels the myth of the neutrality of rules. Discussions about what the law is or what it says contribute mightily to a limiting of the scope of politics, which has grave consequences for a healthy democracy.[10]

Unlike a typical Lockean, I assume a robust and integral conception of citizenship to be the fundamental building block for democratic theory and for a democratic polity. Entailed within this view is the notion that the basic political data of human existence is an initially related membership in a political society. Physical and psychological separateness should neither logically nor historically lead one to an atomistic, nonpolitical metaphysics. The exception occurs when, as was the case with Lockean liberalism, the intention is to create a defense for something, such as private property. My position, again in opposition to the Lockean one, does not appreciate or hold the separation of public and private spheres to be natural, inherently necessary for freedom or liberty, or sacred because of an antisocial metaphysics. For the Lockean, democracy pertains to a pinched perception that politics has only to do with government, indeed, with restricting government. In my view, politics extends far beyond the system of government to embrace social life as well. (This view is quite within the "way of life" democratic tradition of John Dewey.)

Democratic citizenship as seen from this "way of life" viewpoint begins with the notion that enhancing the quality of life and enhancing human potential within society are what ultimately matter and are the templates for political action. Government has a crucial and positive role to play and is not by nature an alien force or factor for achieving goals and pursuits. Politics and being a public person are, as Plato and Aristotle held them to be, integral elements of being human.

Equality is at the core of such a full democratic citizenship perspective. Its importance is underscored in any discussion or practice of discretionary behavior in decision making and implementation. The basic proposition is that all citizens are to be viewed as being qualitatively equal as human beings; as an idea this is not new, but as a goal it is yet to be achieved.[11]

Dworkin makes a very useful distinction between "treatment as an equal" and "equal treatment." "Treatment as an equal," according to him, "is the right, not to receive the same distribution of some burden or benefit, but to be treated with the same respect and concern as anybody else."[12] Along these lines Benn and Peters point out that "what we really demand, when we say that all men are equal, is that none shall be held to have a claim to better treatment than another, in advance of good grounds being produced."[13] The point is that equality does not necessarily mean treating everyone the same or in an identical manner.

If good grounds can be produced, then one could treat or relate differently to different people while at the same time upholding the principle of equality. As criteria for selecting legitimate grounds for different yet equal treatment, I submit the following general standards, which I associate with being standards for a democratic policy:

1. The grounds must square with the notion that all persons are citizens. Even though they may well have differing capacities or abilities, at any one time all have the potential and the right to contribute to society and to receive fair rewards as a result of social membership.
2. As John Rawls put it with his famous difference principle, "The social order is not to establish and secure the more attractive prospects of those better off unless doing so is to the advantage of those less fortunate...."[14]
3. The grounds for making differential distinctions must be publicly advocated, argued, adopted, and followed; and the criteria of accessibility to decision makers, responsiveness to citizen inputs, and decision-making responsibility should obtain.[15] The initial two standards (1 and 2) must be met in order for these more narrow criteria to be legitimately operational.

This position, incidentally, is not one that has antecedents only in antiquity. It is quite similar to a viewpoint associated with those who could be characterized as the non-Lockean, propolitics liberals, such as John Stuart Mill, T. H. Green, L. T. Hobhouse, and John Dewey. This stand of propolitical liberal thinkers, in reaction to the excesses of laissez faire industrialization and the libertarianism of the Manchester School, proposed that the good life was the proper object of social and political action and that citizenship involved such an expectation.[16]

Some grounds for differential treatment clearly are invalid and illegitimate. Differences in sex, religion, ethnic group, socioeconomic class, or political creed, for example, should constitute legitimate grounds for differential treatment only in the context that these were held to be favorable attributes by those making social decisions and that policy remedies must reflect points (1) and (2).

This proposed framework for democratically evaluating policies requires a substantive evaluation of policy results, including a look at anticipated and final results in individual cases. Such an individualization of the decision-making process, while it should enhance the democratic quality of administrative behavior, particularly by allowing for more responsibility to be noticed and assessed, is a radical departure from what occurs presently.

It is most common today to find three arguments packaged under one wrapper and used to defend the present modes of policy implementation, particularly in the area of the law implementation system. One argument, the notion of establishing and "following" rules, already has been considered. A second is the efficiency argument. Essentially this argument holds that there is neither the time nor the energies available to look into each case individually and in its entirety. The third argument is that treating people equally means treating people in similar situations similarly. This last point is an especially attractive one because it reinforces the first—rules can be generated to cover general classes of cases and situations—and it provides a theoretical rationale that helps obscure the explanatory problems of the second—it is difficult to make "easy" or "convenient" into virtues. By defining *equal* in an administratively comfortable fashion (that is, "to treat everyone alike"), history, sociology, economics, and politics are "avoided in formulating policies," usually to the great benefit of those already ascendant as a result of these factors.

Suppose, for example, two families are burned out of their respective homes. One family has the resources sufficient to adequately care for itself in both the short and long runs. The other family is left devastated, both at the moment and for the predictable future (unless the next day they were to win a lottery, perhaps). You have a total of ten units of assistance to disperse; the question is, how can it fairly be distributed? Certainly providing each family five units, treating them equally in the administrative sense, would not be the same in terms of results as treating them as equals. Only differential treatment effected through the exercise of discretion can accomplish the desired democratic objective of creating a fair set of conditions wherein each family can develop and thrive.

Justice blind to the human facts of a case runs a very great risk of being blind justice. Or, as Dickens suggests in *Oliver Twist,* the law has the very great potential of being "an ass." Anatole France's observation about the significant differences between a person stealing a loaf of bread to feed his/her family and the affluent bread thief is most telling on this point. The proper perspective is that of Aristotle: treating unequals in the same manner is as unjust as treating those who are equal in an unequal fashion. Only through the operation of discretionary decision making, as evaluated by democratic standards, can the objective of fairness be achieved.

What we must strive for politically are assurances that public officials will be as impartial and as open as possible in their deliberations and that in exercising discretion officials should apply criteria compatible with the purposes of a democratic society. The nature of such assurances is associated far more with the operation of responsibility, responsiveness, and accountability, than with generating more rules or exercising more "professional behavior" (whatever that means). Such assurances as I have proposed preserve the linkage so important in a democratic environment between those who make public policy and those for whom the policies must be made.

The case for a strong, prevailing democratic presence in discretionary decisions involves considerably more than enumerating certain forms of acceptable or unacceptable behavior. The democratic presence in discretionary decision making provides a political posture and an evaluative environment. It is not the administration of a specific set of rules.

Is politics enough of a check? It is not only enough, but in a democratic mold it is the legitimate one. So long as we have the opportunity to apply democratic criteria, political action is not only enough of a check upon tyranny, it is a better solution to the discretionary dilemma than is generating more rules and retreating from realization of the essentially political nature of the problem. It is better, furthermore, because it places the public decision making where it ought to be, in the political arena.

People such as Davis and Lowi have proposed that just behavior can occur only through establishment of just laws. My political response to such proposals is reinforced by looking at some of the general literature on public administration, public policy, and political theory.[17] According to Edwards and Sharkansky, for example, "each policy arena may be characterized by its own political culture."[18] What prevents democratic standards and values from being applicable to the exercise of discretion across the law system is not, when seen in this light, something inherent or natural about the law, but rather something about our half-willed political commitment to and the real incompleteness of democracy in America. More open politicization—that is, more discretion openly exercised—can and should lead to a more democratic polity. At least politics is worth a try. The other options—administration and liberalism—have proven themselves incapable of success.

CHAPTER TWO

The Politics of Discretionary Justice among Criminal Justice Agencies

WILLIAM C. LOUTHAN

THE CONCEPT of discretion in the criminal justice process has long enjoyed the appreciation of practitioners and the attention of scholars. Both the practice of discretion and regard for the concept of discretion have a long history. Negotiation and bargaining in the justice system are not new; at least some of the forms of discretion have been officially approved; and discretion has been well-researched.[1] Nevertheless, there exists little, if any, consensus on the precise contours of the concept of discretion, on causes for increases or decreases in the exercise of discretion, on the currencies of exchange between and among those criminal justice participants who play at the game of discretion, on the functions discretion performs (empirically derived), or on the benefits discretion produces (normatively judged).

The official exercise of broad discretion in the disposition of cases is at least as old as the American colonial experience. Perhaps this should not be surprising since the American office of public prosecutor was modeled on the traditional system of private criminal litigation in England; the American public prosecutor assumed the role of the British private prosecutor, and just as the private prosecutor had discretion whether or not to prosecute, so the public prosecutor was vested with the same discretion.[2] Although the phenomenon of "plea bargaining" was not yet a formal process, "procedures were personalized and suited to individual criminals as well as to particular categories of crime."[3] About one-third of the cases filed vanished when charges were dropped.[4] Further, juries exercised great discretion in arriving at their verdicts (sometimes, for example, lowering the estimated value of stolen goods in order to find the defendant guilty of petty rather than grand larceny), and judges exercised great discretion in sentencing, reflecting again an "individualized" form of justice (sometimes, for example, handing down penalties not even provided for by law). That such "deviations" from the "rule of law" were thought even then to have had some normatively beneficial effect is

William C. Louthan, Ohio Wesleyan University, Delaware, Ohio.

evidenced by Thomas Jefferson's defense of "the right of a jury to invoke community sentiment and to either disregard the law or the instructions of a judge."

Discretion has remained ever since. When states began passing "habitual criminal" statutes during the last third of the nineteenth century, prosecutorial discretion effectively nullified the intent of the laws by not indicting habitual criminals as such. Turn-of-the-century experiments with what we would now call "diversion programs" (for example, Cleveland's Sunrise Court), effectively transferred an enormous amount of discretionary power to chiefs of police. The "new penology" of early–twentieth century reformers that advocated, inter alia, indeterminate sentences and parole greatly enlarged the effective discretion exercised by both judges and parole boards.

One result of all this was the unprecedented entrance in 1955 of the American Bar Foundation into social science research aimed at describing five key "decision points": detection of crime, arrest, prosecution, adjudication, and sentencing. The findings should not have been surprising. The justice process consists of "a long sequence of discretionary decision-making that. . .[is] both hidden from public view and largely ungoverned by any standards or guidelines."[5] Such conclusions have in turn had at least three results: (1) they have molded the criminal justice "reform" movement into one largely consumed with "bringing discretionary decision-making under control"; (2) they have led to an increasing number of lawsuits challenging the operations of agencies and the behaviors of official participants who allegedly engage in discretionary activities that are "arbitrary" and/or "capricious"; and (3) they have stimulated further research on discretion and its effects.

Nevertheless, there is little agreement on what discretion really is, or on whether its effects are in general deleterious, salutary, or merely benign. For some, discretion is "law without order," "the authority to make decisions according to one's own judgment. . .," the "departure from legal rules"; in short, "normlessness."[6] Others, though, would contend that while discretion may refer to a procedural context of decisions reached informally, it does not necessarily imply that decisions are made on an ad hoc basis, without order, and without reference to some kind of directional norm. Indeed, it can be argued that discretionary behavior itself becomes routine, that the environment of decision is one in which the actor thinks as much (maybe simultaneously, maybe first) about the norms or folkways of discretion and its related currencies of informal exchange as he does about what may be required by the rule of law.

Those who hold to the former view (that discretion begins where rules leave off) also tend to view the effects of discretion negatively, arguing that discretion leads to random capriciousness at minimum and very possibly to patterns of favoritism and discrimination as well.[7] Those who hold to the latter view (that discretion is an informal but routine form of individualized justice) also tend to view the effects of discretion positively, arguing that discretion produces a degree of flexibility in the justice system that is as crucial to our notions of fairness as are the principles of due process and equal protection.[8] Further, on the negative side, there is the argument that discretion is the principal contributor to fragmentation among criminal justice agencies. Here the police-courts-corrections complex is seen as an "arena in which criminal justice participants, each with differing perceptions of crime and corrections, play out their rules in accordance with unscrutinized values and inarticulate objectives" producing, virtually, a "nonsystem."[9] On the other side is the view that the criminal justice system, however fragmented it may be, does possess at least one inescapable "systems" characteristic, namely, interdependence. Here the argument is that the police-courts-corrections complex is an institutionalized setting (analogous to a market) in which participants occupy boundary-spanning roles; they exchange cues, recommendations, refusals, bargains, threats, and resources between and among agencies, ultimately producing both contest (because the power of participants depends largely upon their ability to create favorable clientele relationships in an arena of scarce resources) and cooperation (because the participants' agencies are interdependent subunits).

CAUSES AND EFFECTS: THE RELATIONSHIPS AMONG CRIMINAL JUSTICE PARTICIPANTS

There have, of course, been many attempts to explain the "causes" of discretion in the justice system. Some have concluded that discretion has resulted from "the need to adopt a system created for a rural society to the realities of Urban America that overload the system with cases," thus reflecting "the adaptation of the system to the personal and organizational needs of the administrators."[10] Others argue that a change has occurred in the relationship between rules and discretion as a result of the shift in the organizational character of the administration of justice from the traditional to the bureaucratic.[11] The "traditional" system is one in which official conduct is legitimated by the sanctity of custom, the personage of the judge, and an administrative staff selected by the judge. The "bureaucratic" system is one in which written rules replace custom, civil service replaces personal appointment of administrative staff, and specialists administer the justice bureaucracy in accordance with written procedures and regulations.

Although discretion exists in both systems, it is necessary in the traditional setting when rules "leave off" (no longer providing a guideline under the circumstances), while in the bureaucratic setting discretion is spread through the vast administrative machinery. The traditional problem of "arbitrary decisions" remains in the bureaucratic environment—although such decisions are usually smaller and less visible—but it has changed in the sense that discretion is now necessary not only when rules "leave off," but is especially important in applying the rules themselves. This is because ambiguity results from a complex system in which anonymous specialists gather information, place it in files, and send it to the next office, and in which no one knows exactly who has applied a rule or at what point it was applied. Perhaps all this is to say nothing more than what has been said by those who take a longitudinal approach: "Discretionary decision-making is a constant theme in the history of American criminal justice...." "The amount of discretion has neither increased nor decreased, but has largely moved from one agency to another."[12] In short, discretion removed from one time (historically) or one place (bureaucratically) in the criminal justice system tends to reappear elsewhere in the system. *It is not possible to assume that any outcome is truly mandatory.*

Virtually all commentators appear to agree that, whatever the causes of discretion and whether or not its effects are justifiable (and there is some tendency to equate the inevitability of its causes with justifications for its effects), discretion must exist. Regarding the police, for example, there will always be a general problem of control. Police, like other people, are not always willing to submit completely to the will of their superiors, tending instead to set their own pace and to defend their own mistakes. More particularly, the patrolman sees himself as a person able to make on-the-spot decisions, not as a bureaucratic functionary. The police organization, ordinarily unable to specify overall objectives, is more interested in efficiency than in purpose, while the patrolman would remain unable to demonstrate devotion to the "rational ends" of the bureaucratic organizations of which he is apart, even if such ends were clear.[13]

Certainly, the status and scope of the substantive criminal law is of little assistance. No attempt to formulate substantive criminal codes clearly encompassing all conduct intended to be criminal and excluding all other conduct has ever succeeded. Of course, not even the most carefully drafted code could anticipate every situation that might arise, but that fact neither justifies nor makes inevitable either poor draftsmanship or the failure to revise criminal laws so as to eliminate obsolescence. Ambiguity and overbreadth in turn produce such a variety of prohibitions that priorities of enforcement must be assigned, a task made no easier by the absence of guidelines any less ambiguous.[14]

Obviously, even within a framework of full enforcement, someone must make an initial decision regarding the probable success of a prosecution (based, presumably, on such factors as the sufficiency of the evidence and whether or not the facts as known fall within a rule of law). But there *are* considerations unique to a given defendant that may legitimate a decision not to prosecute. For example, perhaps the offense occurred within the context of a quarrel in which all parties are equally at fault, or the offense is a mere technical violation of the law and a warning suffices to prevent a second infraction. Virtually all commentators would agree, however, that if white-collar crime is treated with leniency while similar crimes of the lower classes are prosecuted pertinaciously, then discretion is being abused. Notice, however, that such abuse is not necessarily the direct result of exercising discretion rather than applying the rule of law. Rather, the essence of the abuse is that individual cases, substantially alike, are being treated differently without justification.

Presumably, there has been some movement in the courtroom itself away from judicial discretion in the interpretation of the rules themselves and toward a greater judicial role in monitoring the behavior of criminal justice participants. Rather than acting as a formal adjudicator of cases, the judge has become a processor of disputes. This is said to be a movement away from formalism because the judge's job now is to move the business of the courts, not to decide cases. He is said to be no longer an adversary umpire, but a process manager.[15] Still, the judge does have a great deal of discretion in deciding whether or not to incarcerate and in determining the length of sentences. Further, the decision to deny probation normally is not reviewable; decisions on early release are made administratively; and the discretion thus exercised is also beyond review.

It could be said in response, however, that waning respect for the rehabilitative ideal and increasing recidivist rates have led us away from the indeterminate sentence. Indeed, many commentators are beginning to notice other limitations on or reductions in the exercise of discretion. Some of these may be seen as systemic. For example, it has been observed that the patrolman's discretion has been reduced by the installation of central data processing systems to report crimes, dispatch officers, and record dispositions. While such systems may both improve reporting methods and add to the "crime rate," they also induce the patrolman to institute formal procedures. Also, the apparently increasing utilization of internal intelligence networks to control police corruption associated with discretion has produced greater centralized control over at least some types of arrest situations. Similarly, there may be systemic limitations on the prosecutor's discretion (to charge and plea bargain) resulting from formal legal rules of discovery by which the case file must be made available to the defense counsel.[16]

Nevertheless, if every violation of the law were prosecuted, the cost would be beyond measure. More important, the absence of formal due process appears to be *preferred* by nearly all criminal justice agencies and participants, *especially by defendants*.[17] This may at first seem strange in a nation "ruled by law" and in which formal procedures have been created to ensure decisions made in accordance with that law. But we are also a nation that believes in justice, and any system committed to the promotion of individualized justice as a matter of principle must also allow for the use of discretion. For example, it is not at all clear that criminal defendants are always better off in a formalized, law-bound environment. Indeed, the defendant's best strategy may not be to maximize due process by securing legal trappings, but to minimize the time and money spent dealing with a court. The real costs to the defendant may not be fines and sentences, but bail bond commissions, attorney fees, and loss of wages. There appears to be little disagreement between prosecutors and defense attorneys that the pretrial process is commonly sufficient to "teach the defendant a lesson."

In short, although the word discretion may suggest to some critics the idea that decisions are arbitrary or capricious, or even discriminatory, the word, in fact, is little more than a reference to a variety of complicated matters associated with the obligation of criminal justice agencies and participants to conform to some set of rules. It is entirely possible for those rules to be nothing more than informal routine norms; and it is possible for those norms to be fair if they result in similar cases being treated similarly. Increasingly, the evidence suggests that bargaining is the dominant mode by which cases are processed at all stages and all levels of the criminal justice system; and that while there may be a unique configuration of actors, strategies, and currencies at each stage, bargaining is "cumulative" and there is a "highly structured understanding of reality and a settled prescription...for action...."[18]

If the severity of the penalty is increased, police may reduce the number of arrests for offenses subject to the penalty, prosecutors may reduce the number of charges for that category of offense, convictions may decrease or, if there are convictions, judges may not fully apply the penalty.[19] If an offender is imprisoned with an indeterminate sentence, parole boards may take into consideration crimes alleged in initial police reports (but never officially charged or tried). Thus, law enforcement personnel may extend their influence to sentencing.[20] If the prosecutor "overcharges," he is merely stating the "asking price" for subsequent bargaining. The overcharge may be intended to induce the defendant to plead guilty to a less serious charge, or to develop informants (that is, an exchange for information), or to reward a defendant by enabling him to confess to a number but not all of the offenses, thus resulting in the "clearance" of many cases. Obviously, all this requires the prosecutor's support for such offers, and usually prosecutors support the offer to maintain cordial relations with local police. In short, there are expected, anticipated, essentially routinized elements of cooperation among police, prosecutors, and defense attorneys. The process may not be formal, but neither is it anarchic or ad hoc. It is characterized by routine within recognized categories of behavioral responses.

In summary, discretion has been a constant theme, both in theory and in practice, in the politics of criminal justice in America. It has won the appreciation of practitioners and the attention of scholars. It has been thought to have at least some beneficial effects, when judged normatively, since the days of Jefferson. The tendency in the most recent literature is away from the empirical description of discretion as law without order (normlessness) and away from the normative judgment that its effects are generally deleterious. Increasingly the tendency is to recognize that, while *discretion* may refer to a procedural context of decisions reached informally, it does not necessarily imply that decisions are made on an ad hoc basis, without order and without reference to some kind of guiding norm. Indeed, the informal processes of negotiation, bargaining, strategies, and currencies of exchange among participants ("asking prices," "real costs," "bargaining limits," "discount factors," and "sentencing payoffs") are viewed increasingly as the anticipated, indeed routine, behavioral practices.

In short, folkways of discretion provide the directional norms that guide behavior at least as often and as routinely as do formal rules of law. Associated with this empirical description is the normative judgment that discretion can and often does produce that degree of flexibility in the justice system crucial to the implementation of our rather well-accepted notions valuing individualized justice and fairnesss.

CHAPTER THREE

The Politics of
Police Discretion

GREGORY   HOWARD   WILLIAMS

TO BEGIN to understand the politics of police discretion it is important to look at not only the way the police themselves determine arrest policies but the way other institutions and agencies of government, such as the legislatures, prosecutors, and local governing bodies, can and do influence arrest policies. Frequently, the role of these other institutions has been overlooked in the analysis of police discretion. Yet state legislatures enact the criminal laws that are to be enforced, prosecutorial offices decide which of the cases brought by the police will be prosecuted, and local governing bodies fund and are politically responsible for local law enforcement decisions. The governor and the state attorney general by virtue of their political positions can undoubtedly exert influence over local police agencies. However, such influence depends more upon their power of persuasion than their explicit legal authority. A governor who has sufficient political influence in the state legislature could bring about the enactment of legislation to control police discretion should he or she desire to do so.[1] The lack of such action in the past, however, suggests there is unlikely to be any change in the future, barring unforeseen developments.[2] While recent court cases and growing civil rights interest group activity may well signify a change from the past, it seems unrealistic to expect that the issue of police discretion will become in most states an issue of major concern on the part of the courts, the governor, or the attorney general.[3]

It seems likely that if any action will be taken, it will be by those institutions, such as the legislatures, prosecutorial offices, local governing bodies, and the police themselves. Thus, it is appropriate to gain an understanding of the ability of those institutions and agencies to influence and control police discretion—specifically arrest decisions.

LEGISLATURES

The major obstacle to formal action to control officers' arrest decisions, according to Kenneth Culp Davis, is that state legislative commands are ambigu-

Gregory H. Williams (former law enforcement officer), Professor, College of Law, University of Iowa, Iowa City.

19

ous.[4] They speak with three voices. First, according to Davis, the legislatures enact state statutes that seemingly mandate full enforcement of the laws. Second, the legislatures provide only enough resources for limited enforcement, and finally, they acquiesce in such partial enforcement. The assessment of legislative action or inaction frequently does not go beyond this analysis. Few writers have asked why legislatures have taken such an approach. There has been no analysis of the extent of legislatures' legal and political authority to provide policy directives, what kind of policy directives it might be realistic to expect the legislatures to produce, or the practical and policy reasons motivating the legislatures to take the approach they have.

Legal and Political Authority. While the power of the U.S. Congress to enact penal legislation is limited to the express provisions of the U.S. Constitution or action that can be accomplished under the "necessary and proper" clause of the Constitution, state legislatures generally have broad power and authority to enact criminal laws. This power is normally authorized under what is referred to as the police power of the state to regulate its internal affairs for the protection of health, safety, and public welfare.[5] The primary limitations on the state's power to enact criminal statutes are federal and state constitutional provisions that protect specific individual rights.

Thus, as long as the state legislatures avoid enacting legislation that would unconstitutionally infringe on an individual's rights, they have a relatively free hand to enact criminal legislation. Because of the nature of the state legislative institution, simply having the power to act does not mean that action is automatically forthcoming.

Legislative Action. Exactly what have the state legislative bodies done to control police discretion? Observation of the work of state legislatures suggests there are several different ways attention can be directed toward controlling police discretion. To assess the importance legislatures place upon the issue of police discretion, it is necessary to attempt to determine the extent to which the topic has arisen on its own as the subject of specific legislative action, has surfaced as a supplement to other legislation, and, finally, has been considered during major revisions of the state criminal codes.

Research indicates that specific legislative proposals to control police discretion are virtually nonexistent. Nor have real concerns about police discretion arisen as part of other legislation. The so-called full enforcement statutes are a prime example of the degree of inattention given to police discretion problems when the issue is a minor part of other noncriminal law legislation. Many statutes calling for full enforcement frequently were part of legislation primarily concerned with establishing local police departments, sheriffs' offices, or state departments of public safety; in the drafting of that legislation much greater consideration was given to the establishment of such agencies than to the establishment of duties of law enforcement officers.[6]

Except in a crisis atmosphere, the primary way in which criminal law legislation has come before state legislatures is through major criminal code revision.

This is a rare undertaking. In the past two decades approximately half the states have revised their criminal codes.[7] When such revision has been undertaken, it has generally provided the opportunity for states to address the broader issues of criminal law—such as police discretion—rather than engaging in the ad hoc formulation of criminal law legislation, which is the norm.[8] The primary focus of most criminal code revision is to simplify statutory language, remove archaic and ambiguous provisions, incorporate case law into the statutes, classify and grade offenses.[9]

Of the states that have undertaken criminal code reform, a substantial proportion have or had full enforcement statutes.[10] A review of the criminal code revisions of those states shows, in spite of the concerns that have been expressed about full enforcement legislation, there has been little effort to repeal or modify the statutes. There are two exceptions. Iowa in 1977 and Kentucky in 1970 did repeal their full enforcement statutes during revision of the state criminal code. In Iowa, however, interviews with legislators indicate that the repeal of the full enforcement legislation was more inadvertent than directed at addressing problems of police discretion.[11]

Nonetheless, to truly understand the legislative approach to police discretion, we must also review other possible legislative action that bears on police discretion, such as efforts by the legislature to limit discretion on vague and ambiguous statutes about vagrancy and disorderly conduct, or to decriminalize such actions; the extent to which the statutes provide policy guidance for law enforcement and anticipate the exercise of limited discretion; and the extent to which the legislature has placed specific limitations on the discretion of other actors in the criminal justice system.

Additional information about the legislative approach to discretion is provided by an analysis of statues typically considered "vague," focusing on laws that permit police officers to issue a citation and summons rather than to physically arrest law violators, since such statutes are a clear legislative indication that the police are expected to exercise some discretion as to how individuals are processed through the system. The extent to which the use of deadly and nondeadly force is proscribed provides another dimension by which to gauge legislative interest in controlling discretion of officers.

To gain some basic understanding of the legislative approach toward discretion of the state legislatures, several states that have substantially revised their criminal codes in the past twenty years were analyzed.[12] Some interesting information emerges. First, a look at the full enforcement statutes shows a remarkable lack of interest in repealing that legislation.

Repeal of the full enforcement statutes, however, is not even the best or the most appropriate way to deal with the problem of police discretion. A better way is to provide more flexible and workable statutes for law enforcement officers. This can be accomplished by remedying problems of vagueness and overbreadth and by decriminalizing statutes that are largely unenforceable or not expected to be enforced.

In a few states there was concern about the overbreadth of some criminal statues in that "the very presence of such broadsweeping provisions on the statute books may in itself place a needless burden on local police."[13] To resolve this problem in Michigan, it was suggested that the vagrancy statute be replaced by provisions prohibiting specific acts, such as prostitution, loitering, and disorderly conduct. Those proposing criminal code revision in Michigan felt that while some sections might still suffer from vagueness, the narrowing of laws such as those on vagrancy "should serve both to promote more equal enforcement of the law and to facilitate more efficient police administration."[14]

The point is well taken but raises another issue. Vagrancy is only one source of enforcement problems; other more frequently enforced, low-visibility crimes such as disorderly conduct, public intoxication, and simple assault also must be considered. In fact, one might argue that replacing the law on vagrancy with a disorderly conduct statute creates its own set of enforcement problems. Disorderly conduct statutes themselves have increasingly come under attack as being deficient in meeting constitutional standards.[15] It seems that the approach of the committee that suggested revisions to the Michigan legislature, like others, was to review overbreadth problems in statutes where there was an immediate question of constitutionality and to replace those specific statutes with ones of less questionable constitutional status. For example, recent attacks on the constitutionality of laws regulating private, consensual sexual behavior such as adultery and sodomy have resulted in their repeal. This has been the case in Iowa, Minnesota, and Missouri. However, in most legislatures there has been no attempt to deal directly or across the board with other constitutionally questionable statutes.

Not only has there been little effort to repeal constitutionally questionable statutes that are not the subject of immediate attack, legislatures have not attempted to lay out the policy objectives of statutes to guide officers in enforcement. Recent changes in the Iowa gambling statute are an example. The new Iowa statute permits some form of gambling. While the effort to reinforce the idea that the legislature did not intend to prohibit all gambling was laudable, the lack of guidelines as to what groups qualified for exemption under the Iowa law created serious problems for local police. Legislators indicated their low level of concern about police discretion by making clear that modification to address enforcement problems was very low on the legislative agenda.

Another way to gauge the extent to which state legislatures are concerned with the problems of police discretion is to look at how the legislature has structured police action subsequent to an arrest. Some state legislatures have provided for the citation system, which gives the officer some discretion to decide how violators will be processed through the criminal justice system. In Arkansas the adoption of the citation system was an explicit recognition of the exercise of police discretion.[16] Discretion was permitted at three levels: by the officer in the field, by the supervising officer at the station house, and by that supervising officer acting under the authorization of the prosecuting attorney.

Few states have adopted the citation system, however, and even in states where it was adopted there have been problems. The legislative approach toward the use of citations has been similar to the general approach toward criminal code revision — the proposals go only half way. The legislatures did not give policy guidance as to when citations are to be issued, specifically what crimes are to be citable, and how officers should decide who should receive a citation. The Arkansas statute provides a list of criteria to consider before issuing the citation, but no direction is given on what crimes are citable.[17] The Iowa citation statute gives no direction on who should be cited but does give some limited direction on what crimes are citable.[18] Neither statute followed the suggestion of the American Law Institute and required the police to issue administrative regulations to control the issuance of citations; nor did either state make the issuance of citations mandatory in certain crimes, such as simple misdemeanors.[19] The end result is that while the citation statutes on their face recognize and expect police discretion, the problems of implementation obviously were given little consideration.

Another way to determine legislative concern about police discretion is to analyze statutes concerning the use of deadly force. Several of the states reviewed had addressed the issue. In fact, nationwide a majority of the states have specific provisions governing the use of deadly force.[20] Approximately twenty-four states have codified the common-law "fleeing felon" rule under which a law enforcement officer is justified in using deadly force in order to arrest any person suspected of committing any felony.[21] Primarily because of the considerable discretion inherent in the choice to use deadly force, provisions of the Model Penal Code have called for state statutes requiring the decision to use deadly force be based on the concern for immediate public safety rather than the fact that a felony, in name only, has been committed.[22]

As a general proposition, efforts to control the use of deadly force have not fared too well over time. For example, the Missouri legislature rejected the suggestion of its advisory committee to limit the use of deadly force to those situations where an individual has committed a felony "involving the use or threatened use of physical force against a person."[23] The statute as passed by the Missouri legislature permits an officer to use deadly force when he or she "reasonably believes" such force is necessary. Of the states evaluated, over half dealt with the issue of the use of force, but few adhered to the standard of the Model Penal Code concerning the police decision to use force. The approach of the legislatures evaluated has to be described as one of maintaining extensive discretion in the use of force—not of limiting it.

A final way to gauge state legislative attitudes toward police discretion is to evaluate the manner in which other discretionary aspects of the criminal justice system have been treated in criminal code revision. The findings here are striking. Many code revisions have focused on the need to control judicial discretion, especially in sentencing.[24] The concern is motivated by the problem of disparate sentencing. For example, in Arizona efforts at criminal code revision were largely motivated by public distress about the unfair sentencing procedures of the old code. Such concern provided a major impetus for revision of the entire criminal code.[25]

Under Arizona's former criminal code, sentences were prescribed individually in each statute defining an offense. The range of sentences permitted was broad, apparently to allow the courts power to shape the punishment of offenders to enhance their rehabilitation. Such discretionary power, however, caused widespread disparity in sentencing. The new code classified each offense, and specific punishment was provided for each class.[26] The range of punishment for each class was sharply limited, consistent with the purposes of retribution and deterrence emphasized as punishment goals by the code.

Arizona also adopted the increasingly popular approach of presumptive sentencing that established minimum, maximum, and normative sentences for offenders. While individual judges may, within certain ranges, raise or lower penalties and thus depart from the presumptive sentence, such departure requires justification.[27]

The efforts of the Arizona legislature to control the sentencing discretion of judges is typical of a large proportion of the states reviewed. Every state reviewed attempted in one way or another to limit sentencing discretion. Two conclusions about such action are warranted: first, the state legislatures have acted on some discretionary problems in the criminal justice system; second, such action seems to occur largely because of public awareness and concern about the excesses of such discretion.

A review of the indices used to gauge legislative action on police discretion indicates there has been some limited action on police discretion and related issues. Such action can be characterized as ambiguous at best, however, and it has been neither sustained nor uniform. Some legislatures have repealed the full enforcement laws, but apparently not because there was a concern with problems of police discretion. Others addressed some enforcement problems in ambiguous criminal statutes, but that work has been very limited. There has been no significant legislative focus on the substantive problems of police enforcement of the criminal laws. Control of the police has clearly not been an institutional priority.

PROSECUTORIAL OFFICES

The political and legal position of prosecutors with respect to police rule making is different from that of the legislatures. The prosecutors' statutory role as a clearinghouse for selecting cases to be prosecuted would, at least on the surface, appear to give them substantial input into police decision making.[28] Nonetheless, there has been very little involvement or even discussion of the role of prosecutors in influencing police arrest policies. A significant unanswered question is why prosecutors haven't been more directly involved in police decision making.

In at least one state, limited interviews indicate police discretion is not an issue of major concern to prosecutors. When selected prosecutors in Iowa were asked to identify the "major criminal justice issues that confront" the state, police discretion was not once identified. Even when the issue of police discretion was identified, it continued to rank toward the lower end of the priority scale. Why does the issue of police discretion have such low priority? While the personality of the prosecuting attorney unquestionably has a significant influence over whether issues are important or not, it seems that the major reasons for the low priority of police discretion are largely institutionally based. The institutional features of the office serve to limit the significance of the problem and the impetus to deal with it directly.

First, there exists a problem of lower-level separation of powers, or, more accurately, a separation of function dilemma. Police and prosecutors have overlapping functions, which include making arrest decisions, but there is a tradition against close oversight of police arrest policies. The limited review may be attributable to the fact that most prosecutors are elected officials—separate and distinct political entities from local law enforcement agencies.[29] Even in states where prosecutors are appointed it is rare for those who appoint prosecutors to have a similar power to appoint local police executives. Thus the police and prosecutors are quite likely to have very different political constituencies, which may be reflected in their enforcement policies.

A second and more compelling factor may also account for the limited involvement of prosecutors in police arrest decisions. Very simply, prosecutors, in deciding which cases to prosecute, have the authority to overrule police arrest decisions. The prosecutors not only can decide which cases will be prosecuted and which will not, but also have the authority to seek the arrest of those the police have decided not to charge. The proscutor's complete control over which cases will be prosecuted does not give him absolute control over arrest policies and resource allocation decisions of the police, but the power to make decisions on charging substantially lessens the prosecutor's need to be concerned with police discretion in the enforcement of low-visibility crimes.

A third reason for the reluctance of prosecutors to become involved in the development of arrest policy guidelines is a desire not to call excessive attention to the prosecutor's own extensive discretionary powers. It is the prosecutor's prerogative to decide, virtually alone, what laws shall be enforced and what persons shall be brought to court.

Historically, prosecutors have been loath to draw attention to their discretionary powers, apparently because of a feeling the public would be concerned about the extent of that power. Joan Jacoby reports in *The American Prosecutor: A Search for Identity* the considerable public shock that has occurred when the broad discretionary powers of prosecutors have been discovered. Another study also has found that while prosecuting attorneys admit their discretionary power is indeed broad, they are not inclined to discuss it publicly and are prone to focus the discussion on the limitations of that power, even though the explicit limitations are quite rare.[30]

Although the police and the prosecutor perform some overlapping functions, each has generally refrained from intruding on the prerogatives of the other. However, at least as far as the prosecutors are concerned, major institutional impediments to action to deal with police discretion problems are being removed and a new era of cooperation between police and prosecutors may well be under way. Such a development can be expected to have significant implications for the development of police arrest policies. If substantive changes are to be made, however, there needs to be more explicit delineation of the role of prosecutors in aiding the formulation of police enforcement policies. As a consequence of that need, a more refined development of the institutional relationship between police and prosecutors will be required and some concrete models must be developed.

Vagueness about the exact nature of the police-prosecutor relationship is notable in the police discretion issue. One example is that of Iowa's Polk County attorney's office, which has promoted extensive use of the citation procedures as authorized by state statute. While the Des Moines Police Department did in fact issue guidelines calling for the use of citations in lieu of arrest, a look at those guidelines reveals a different approach taken by the two offices toward the use of citations. Whereas the prosecutors asked the police to exercise their discretionary powers to issue citations, the police acted by developing guidelines controlling the issuance of such citations. Such guidelines do not appear likely to result, and apparently have not resulted, in many citation arrests being made. Because of the different political constituency of each institution (police and prosecutors), neither can force a resolution to this stalemate. A resolution can come only at another level of government—either by the legislature specifically detailing the extent to which prosecutors can require their policy suggestions to be adopted by local police—or by local governing bodies attempting to resolve the problem.

LOCAL GOVERNMENT

Unfortunately, limited local governmental involvement in police affairs is typical nationwide. The Ohio Advisory Committee to the U.S. Commission on Civil Rights suggested in its study of *Policing in Cincinnati, Ohio: Official Policy vs. Civilian Reality* that the failure of city officials to control local police had contributed to many of the problems of police-community relations in that city. Likewise, the Kansas Advisory Committee to the U.S. Commission on Civil Rights felt city officials were remiss in their review of police department practices. Finally, in a national study by the U.S. Commission on Civil Rights in which the central focus was the "institutional mechanisms which impact upon police conduct," a major concern was the lack of "local government oversight" of police activity.[31]

As with prosecutors and legislators, police discretion appears to be a low-priority issue to local government officials. Although there is concern by local government officials that the police exercise their powers of discretion fairly and uniformly, the general feeling is that there is little need for city officials to intervene to ensure such is done. It is the rare situation when city officials feel it is appropriate to question police officials about enforcement policies. The general feeling is that hiring good officers and providing adequate training and departmental supervision obviate the need for the mayor, city manager, or city countil to "run" the police departments.

Undoubtedly the appropriateness of this posture is reinforced in city officials' minds by the lack of organized interest groups such as civil rights organizations pushing for efforts to control police arrest policies. A strongly perceived concern among such interest groups might well change the approach of city officials. Even assuming there is such a change, however, two other factors are strong institutional impediments to action.

First, there is a traditional reluctance to interject partisan politics into the development of law enforcement policy; and second, normal techniques of supervision and evaluation of local administrative agencies do not provide close review of the activities of law enforcement agencies. There is an extensive history in the United States of generally negative results when state and local political officials become involved in law enforcement. Events around the turn of the century, when the involvement of local government officials in the internal operation of police departments was substantial, made it clear that law enforcement decisions were influenced by political decisions.[32] Because of a strong reaction against political influence in law enforcement, the trend since that time has been to make special efforts to ensure that partisan politics has no place in law enforcement. This clearly has been the attitude of the past twenty years in America. Recent studies have found determined effort by local officials to avoid intervention in police department work, particularly in issues concerning development of law enforcement policy.[33]

This attitude is consistent with the findings of limited interviews across Iowa. The general feeling was that local government control of the police was an "either-or" proposition. Either local officials control the police and politics influences law enforcement policy, or the police are left alone and politics stays out of law enforcement. Even if local government officials are able to overcome the traditional reluctance to monitor and review police activity, another major obstacle must be overcome. Because the responsibilities of the police are fundamentally different from those of other locally oriented administrative agencies, bringing the police under administrative control presents special difficulties in that usual methods of supervision and evaluation are not adequate. Local governing bodies can fairly easily evaluate the work of most municipal agencies because their work is largely ministerial and not discretionary. The various city agencies make recommendations for new sewage treatment plants, additional traffic lights, street pavings, and the like, but the council decides whether the plants will be built, the lights installed, or the streets paved. The agencies then carry out the council's directives and the faithfulness with which they do so can be checked. With regard to the police it is a different story; rarely will the council ask or the police tell them their enforcement priorities, and even less rarely will the council indicate the police are making too many or too few arrests.

Contributing to the lack of review of the police may well be a feeling of lack of expertise on the part of the local officials, a feeling to which the police frequently contribute. This was certainly the attitude of many police agencies when civilian review boards were considered in many cities in the 1960s. The point was frequently made by the police that civilians needed much more expertise in order to evaluate police performance.[34] Surprisingly enough, one finds a number of recent events that indicate a possible change of attitude by local governing bodies. Most significant are recent court decisions that have substantially changed the law on municipal liability.

Traditionally municipalities were not liable for the improper acts of their law enforcement officers. Although the immunity of the state from suit was not directly passed to the local communities, a modified form of immunity developed over the years.[35] This immunity was primarily reflected in the distinction between governmental and proprietary functions.[36] Local governments were liable only for the improper acts of their agents arising out of proprietary functions, such as when the local government was engaging in an activity normally performed in the private sector (for instance, business activities). The view was that if local governments were competing with private enterprise, they should bear the same risks of doing business as do those in the private sector. With regard to governmental functions such as law enforcement, a different approach was followed. In performing governmental functions local governments were motivated primarily by the desire to provide a benefit for society not performed by the private sector. A municipal government generally was immune from suit for the negligent performance of the "governmental" acts by its officers, although individual officers may have been personally liable.

The shield of immunity provided municipalities may be rapidly eroding. The abolition of sovereign immunity in many states and the authorization of suits against cities under federal civil rights statutes increases the likelihood that cities may be held accountable for the discretionary arrest policies of their police officers.[37] Thus institutional changes must occur to avoid costly and prolonged litigation.[38] But what must be the nature of the institutional changes? At first blush one could argue that mayors and city councils could more closely scrutinize police operations, such as resource allocation decisions and police arrest policies. But even if they did, it is not clear that the end result would be substantially different.

Most mayors and city council members are and would likely perceive that they are ill-equipped to engage in the role of overseer. If city officials are to be able to review police operations intelligently, they need to have a basic theory to guide them. At this point there is no systematic way of reviewing the work of the police. No official enforcement policies are articulated, although informal ones clearly are followed. Very simply, there is no way to determine whether the police have performed as expected because no standard of performance has been enunciated. As we have seen thus far, no standards of performance have been developed by the legislatures, prosecutors, or local governing bodies. The final question, then is whether it is realistic to expect any action by the police themselves.

POLICE

Although there has been some discussion of the need for the police to act formally to develop rules controlling police discretion, conspicuously absent in that discussion is treatment of the extent to which institutional obstacles such as the myth of "full enforcement," covert pressure for maintaining the status quo, legal concerns, and the general failure to recognize the police as policymakers might inhibit open and formalized law enforcement policymaking by the police. In considering the development of rules to control police discretion, it is important not only to gain some understanding of why the police have generally resisted the idea of rule development but also to learn whether there are differences within police departments that can impede development and implementation of enforcement policy—how are rules likely to be accepted in police departments; is there likely to be a difference in response between departmental supervisors and patrol officers; and how might that difference affect the rule-making process?

As a general proposition, the police have not been motivated to undertake substantive rule-making. The likely reasons for their reluctance are both political and legal. A major block to action appears to be the myth of full enforcement. The police have imbued themselves with the idea that criminal laws are impartially enforced and that no choices are made in determining whether or against whom the laws will be enforced. General police response has been to carve out an institutional identification as an organization performing mere ministerial functions and not as an administrative agency making policy decisions. Police administrators hide behind a full-enforcement myth rather than face the controversy that would result from attempting to deal with ambiguous statures. Professor Stephen Schiller's work confirms this hypothesis: he states that police administrators refuse to acknowledge the existence of selective enforcement policies because to do so would require them to state the policy and to defend it. By taking positions on discretionary enforcement, they would lose an image of impartiality.[39] Obviously such an attitude by the police will have an impact on both the development and the implementation of guidelines, and it should be confronted. A strategy must be developed to ensure that the implementation of enforcement guidelines permits the police to retain their image as impartial enforcers of the law.

A more practical reason for the reluctance of police to become involved in developing selective enforcement policies appears to be the existence of some unanswered legal questions. For example, development of law enforcement rules may be technically in violation of state law. This not only raises the question of whether an individual charged with violation of the law would be able to attack the validity of the rules, but it also creates some internal problems for the police. How can the police penalize an officer who fails to follow the selective enforcement rules? It would seem relatively easy for an officer charged with a violation of departmental enforcement rules to defend such a charge on the grounds that rules drafted in defiance of full-enforcement legislation are invalid. Yet, if the superiors could not discipline a patrol officer for a violation of the rules, the ability to develop law enforcement policies would be seriously limited.

A more important concern, however, is public knowledge and usage of the guidelines. Indications are that police officials feel such guidelines would be used against the police in litigation of criminal cases. The feeling appears to be that the rules developed to control the exercise of police discretion would be used as a standard by the courts for gauging police conduct, and specifically that the police would be required to show why certain citizens were arrested and others were not, rather than permitting the rules only to be used internally to discipline officers who violate them. James Q. Wilson, like many police chiefs, is concerned that if police develop policy the courts are going to hold them to it.[40]

That has not been the general thrust of recent cases, however. There have been two recent cases, *Chastain v. the Civil Service Board of Orlando* and the *City of St. Petersburg v. Reed,*[41] in which the courts concluded that while local police department regulations controlling the use of deadly force by officers would be appropriate to use in disciplinary proceedings against officers, they would not be controlling in any civil or criminal action arising from an incident in which such force was used.[42] While this has been one case that has held to the contrary, a more important case on the issue was decided by the U.S. Supreme Court. In *United States v. Caceres* the Court decided that evidence obtained in violation of Internal Revenue Service regulations could not be excluded from the criminal trial of a taxpayer.[43] In *Caceres* the Supreme Court indicated it is sufficiently concerned with the need for agencies to control their discretion that it will give that need serious consideration before taking action likely to curb such rule making.

Finally, there is a need to take a close look at how the police as an institution can influence internal attitudes of the police themselves toward rule making. Does the institutional structure influence the attitude toward and likely acceptance of rules? Views differ as to the fundamental nature of the police. Some writers argue that the police are a paramilitary institution and therefore amenable to rule development.[44] Even if they are not paramilitary organizations, police still may "want to be told what to do."[45] The problem, however, is not only whether the patrol officers "want to be told what to do" but whether police officials want to tell the officers what to do. One has to assume that the inverted pyramid of responsibility in which street officers exercise significant discretion in the arrest decision, so frequently referred to in police work, neither occurred nor continues to exist by chance. Assessing the ability to control law enforcement policy requires a broad approach. Proposals to control police discretion are doomed to fail unless police are recognized as policymakers and unless coordinated action is taken to address the basic systemic questions of institutional power and authority.

CHAPTER FOUR

Judicial Discretion in Pretrial Release

FRED RHYNHART

DISCRETION is evident in every stage of the criminal justice process, from the police officer's decision to arrest to the parole board's decision to grant early release from sentence. This was emphasized by the President's Commission on Law Enforcement and Criminal Justice and posed a challenge to researchers in the criminal justice field. The research reported here is the result of inquiry into judicial discretion with respect to bail setting, or pretrial release, and the impact on that decision of a pretrial service agency.

Depending upon the particular jurisdiction, the bail-setting decision may occur immediately after arrest and booking in the station house; at a preliminary hearing or arraignment before a magistrate or first-trial judge; or upon review after a formal indictment. The decision represents a determination whether and on what terms an arrested individual will be allowed to remain in the community between arrest and case disposition. The granting of bond, whether based on surety or signature, permits the accused to continue life within the family, neighborhood, or community, with reasonable assurance that court obligations will be honored. Denial of bond results in imprisonment throughout case disposition.[1]

Discretion is present, as Davis suggests, in any situation in which the effective limits on an official's "power leave him free to make a choice among possible courses of action or inaction." The standards governing bail decisions are reflected in state statutes and criminal codes, but inevitably they leave the decision to the judgment and discretion of the judge. An Ohio statute, for example, defines the purpose of bail as "to insure that the defendant appears at all stages of the criminal proceedings." It goes on to note that "all persons are entitled to bail, except in capital cases where the proof is evident or the presumption great." Thus the availability of bail is a matter of judicial discretion in some instances, and the amount or nature of bail is subject to judicial determination in all cases.[2]

Despite the statutory requirement defining assurance of court appearances as the only legitimate function of bail in most states, research indicates that the

---

Fred Rhynhart, Northern Kentucky University, Highland Heights, and Deputy Judge Executive, Campbell County Kentucky.

courts in fact use bail for a variety of purposes. Freed and Wald suggest that other functions of bail, legitimate or not, include "to prevent a recurrence of criminal conduct by an accused believed to be dangerous to the community; and to punish the accused by giving him a taste of jail." Wice further notes that bail is often used for manipulative purposes, pressuring a defendant to waive the right to an attorney and to secure immediate disposition of a case. These alternative uses of bail reinforce the argument that pretrial release is largely a function of judicial discretion.[3]

THE BAIL SYSTEM AND REFORM

The traditional money bond system, a heritage of English custom and American adaptation, allows a person to purchase his release pending trial. The court determines the amount of bail, and if a defendant cannot provide the bond on his own, he may purchase a bond from a private bondsman. Thus, a second decision is involved: whether the private bondsman will accept the risk and provide support for a defendant. In operation, the system poses two contradictions to the concept of a right to bail, defined in state statutes, and the prohibition on excessive bail, cited in the Eighth Amendment of the U.S. Constitution. First, access to money becomes the determinant of individual rights, because even a very small bail may deny the indigent an opportunity for pretrial release. Second, the private bondsman, not formally associated with the judiciary in any fashion, is in effect given the right to override a judge's decision simply by refusing to provide bail for a defendant.

These contradictions in the theory of bail, and the questionable character of the commercial bail business in practice, became the basis for a reform movement in the 1960s.[4] Alternatives to the money bond were identified and tested, including refundable percentage deposits, property bonds, and personal or signature bonds, commonly called Own Recognizance (OR) bonds. Further, attempts were made to improve the information available at the time of bail setting, usually involving the creation of pretrial service agencies.

The primary impetus for change in the bail system came from the Manhattan Bail Project, which was developed and tested between 1961 and 1964 by the Vera Institute of Justice in the Manhattan Magistrate's Felony Court (later merged with the Court of Special Sessions, New York City).[5] The experiment was duplicated in Des Moines, Iowa, and it became the motivating force for the 1964 National Conference on Bail and Criminal Justice, held in Washington, D.C. Throughout the following decade pilot projects were established across the country, applying the model developed by Vera and consciously seeking to evaluate the impact of such experiments on the bail system.

While modified over time in response to experience, and differing in some respects depending upon the implementing jurisdiction, the bail projects came to reflect a common pattern:

1. Investigators interview defendants as soon as possible after arrest.
2. Information is obtained and verified where possible on defendant's personal character.

3. Recommendations are made at the time of bail setting on eligibility for release on recognizance (ROR).
4. Those granted ROR are supervised to ensure that court obligations are met.

The evaluation over time seems to substantiate the hypothesis posed by the reformers: that variations in money bail were not unnecessarily related to default or jump rates; that a greater number of defendants could be released on signature without jeopardizing case disposition; that bail was not any more effective as a guarantee of court appearance than release on verified information; and that presented with information on individual defendants at the time of bail setting, judges could and would make use of alternatives to the conventional money bond.[6]

This last conclusion frames the research undertaken in Cincinnati and reported here. Given the nature of judicial discretion in the bail-setting decision, what influences the judge in the decision process? The availability of greater options in the bond decision, and of information concerning the individual defendant before the court, in effect increases the discretion of judicial decision makers. The questions posed here include: (1) What criteria influence the bail decision? (2) On what basis do judges choose among the options available? (3) What weight is given to the recommendation of the pretrial service agency?

BAIL REFORM IN OHIO

Advocates of bail reform in Ohio (1973–1974) sought the release of more defendants, many of whom are indigent, on personal recognizance or dollar-free bail. Personal signature was conceived as a method of reducing overcrowded jails and inequities in a system. Structural discretion was the form that the Ohio bail reform took, with Rule 46 of the Criminal Code as its expression. Rule 46 urged that personal recognizance should be used in felonies "unless the judge is convinced that such will not assure appearance for trial."[7] Yet the structural discretion that Rule 46 gave the local trial judges consisted of multiple criteria without a weighting formula. The net result was that this operationalization of structural discretion was sufficiently loose for individual judges to weight the ten factors as they wished. The trial judges were to consider

1. The nature and circumstances of the offense charged
2. The weight of the evidence against the accused
3. The family ties of the accused
4. The employment of the accused
5. Financial resources of the accused
6. The character of the accused
7. The mental condition of the defendant
8. The length of residence of the accused in the community
9. The record of convictions of the accused
10. The record of appearance at previous court proceedings

Only the third, fourth, and eighth factors were related to bail reform. These had been pulled together by the Vera Institute of Justice to make up the Vera Scale, which tried to establish the social and psychological ties of the defendant to the community. The idea was that family, economic, and community ties would be sufficient to keep the overwhelming majority of defendants from fleeing. If this were valid, the bail reformers felt, jail overcrowding and the inequities of freedom based on money could be done away with.

Although the remaining seven factors did not relate to bail reform, they remained in Rule 46. These were the key criteria used by trial court judges in putting their discretion to work in the previous bail-bonding system. They included (1) the seriousness of the charge, (2) the record of the individual, and (3) the evidence on hand.

The operationalization of structural discretion in Rule 46 provided the Vera reform as one approach or consideration that fell within the discretion of local trial court judges. Reformers advocating Rule 46 pushed the Vera reform as *the* legitimate approach. Hartmann, writing in the *University of Cincinnati Law Review*, argued that it would be "difficult for a judge at a preliminary hearing not to give serious consideration to the release of the accused on his own recognizance." Hartmann cited two federal cases as a guiding light for local trial court judges in Ohio. In *Wood v. U.S.*, 391 F2d 981 (1968), the following was argued: "The [federal] Bail Reform creates a strong policy in favor of release on personal recognizance and it is only if such a release would not reasonably assure the appearance as required that other conditions of release may be imposed. In *U.S. v. Bronson*, 433 F2d 537 (1970), the opinion held that "the court must in each case seek the minimal nonfinancial conditions of release which reasonably assures the presence of that particular defendant."

A third federal case, *U.S. v. Cowper*, 33 Ohio Misc 57 (1972), decided in U.S. District Court, Northern Ohio District, reduced the bond set by the federal magistrate for a defendant with a grand larceny charge from $100,000 cash to $50,000 at 10 percent ($5,000). It reduced the bail because the magistrate had not taken into account the accused's employment record and family and residence ties, as well as the lack of a criminal record. Judge Lambros wrote:

> The [federal] Bail Reform Act requires the courts to reexamine pre-trial release practices. In no other field of law is the conflict between reality and legal theory more pronounced. While adhering in theory to the constitutional principle that a person should not be punished until he has been found guilty in a court of law, the courts in this nation have acquiesced to the fact that more than a third of those persons incarcerated on any given day have not been guilty and that pre-trial detainees are jailed in far worse condition than those convicted of crimes.

A fourth federal case, *Workman v. Cardwell*, 31 Ohio Misc 99, U.S. District Court, Northern Ohio District (1972), is of interest because it found three Ohio state courts (common pleas, the court of appeals, and the supreme court) had abused their discretion in setting bail for Workman to the point of denying him equal protection of the laws. In ruling that a bond set at $5,000 for an indigent is excessive bail, the court opinion said:

The setting of bail may not be used as a device for keeping persons in jail upon an indictment pending their trial. Rather it is to enable a defendant to stay out of jail until he has been found guilty while guaranteeing his presence at trial. . . .

If the bail setting of Ohio's trial court judges were to reflect these federal court decisions, then the implementation of Rule 46 would have followed Hartmann's hopeful projection that "release without financial outlay by the accused should become the norm rather than the exception."[8] Yet we should not overlook one important rule laid down by the district court in the Workman case: "This opinion in no way contemplates that the state may not jail a person accused of a crime prior to trial."

This rule recognized that the American federal system limits the practical control the federal courts have over the states' criminal justice systems in reference to bail. In American federalism each state maintains control over its own criminal justice system unless, through the process of appeal, abuses are found. Clearly, every bail decision cannot be reviewed in the federal courts without altering the structure of both the federal court and state systems. As the court noted in *Workman,* bail setting is better left to the states with the hope that "many of the unfortunate practices of the bail system may be remedied [in Ohio] by the adaptation of [the then] proposed Rule 46 of the Ohio Rules of Criminal Procedure." This is consistent with American federalism in trying to keep as many decisions as close as possible to the grass roots, with the federal courts acting as a safety valve if local practices deny individual rights.

Reform, if it is to have effect, must be implemented. Rule 46, a multiple-criteria, structural discretion system, was implemented into an ongoing ethos, or system. This is doubly important because the implementation of the ten criteria of Rule 46 was up to the discretion of local trial-court judges. These judges, trained in the law, had been socialized in and had received their legal experience in a state that previously had not included the elements of the Vera reform as criteria for bail setting.

Until implementation of Rule 46, the Ohio Constitution, statutes, and case law had set out a wide structural zone of discretion to those trial judges that set bail. Section 9, Article 1, of the Ohio Constitution sets forth that "excessive bail shall not be required" as one guidepost for this discretion. The statutes (before Rule 46) and case law gave three critiera for consideration by local judges:

1. The nature of the offense
2. The associated penalty
3. The probability of guilt

In *Ohio v. Richardson,* 15 Ohio Opinion 461 (1939), the court noted the difficulty of balancing the state constitution with statutes and case law:

> The great difficulty arises as to what is reasonable and what may be excessive. Ultimately it seems it resolves itself into a question of the exercise of

sound discretion by the court in each individual case depending upon all of the facts and circumstances surrounding each individual case.

In re Polizzi, 61 Ohio App 354 (1939), the court of appeals argued the determination of excessive bail should be made by the trial court, not the appeals court. The court stated that "for us [an appeals court] to make an order different from that of the trial court would simply be a substitution made without adequate data."

Limits were placed on the trial court in *In re Lonardo,* 86 Ohio Appelate Reports 289 (1949), a case in which $75,000 bail for vagrancy was found on appeal to be excessive. In this case the court noted, "A criminal may have forfeited his right to liberty but neither do courts nor any other power have the right to deprive him of it except in accordance with the law of the land." The court ruled that bail worth many times the dollar value of the penalty—750 times the dollar value of the fine in this case—was unreasonable and excessive. Even in this case, oft cited for the limits it put on local trial court discretion, it should be noted that bail was reduced by a factor of 5 to be reset at $15,000—still 150 times the dollar value of the fine imposed. *In re Lonardo* set out the theoretical principle of excessive bail as a basis for review, but it reinforced the principle of local discretion by maintaining bail much greater than the dollar value of the penalty associated with the charge.

The principle of local discretion was set out in *Hampton v. State,* 42 OS 401 (1884). The court held the trial court could set bail in ways it thought appropriate, even after conviction prior to sentencing. The court wrote, "The power to admit bail is amply given to the courts and is incidental and necessary to the due administration of justice; and this power is not taken away until the prisoner found guilty of a felony has been sentenced."

The philosophy of local trial courts is best summarized in *Valentine v. Smith,* 8 026 (1837). This opinion argued that "every court does its duty and does right...." The local trial court was "the judge of its weight, its credibility, and although its conclusion may have been different from what ours would have been called to decide on the same evidence had we been called to decide on the same evidence, its decision was a subject of sound discretion."

The only practical limit on a local trial court's discretion is an outright denial of Section 9, Article 1, of the Ohio Constitution, which states that bail must be set save for capital offenses. Grand larceny, receiving and concealing stolen property, and burglary were pointed out by the Ohio Supreme Court (*Locke v. Jenkins,* 20 Ohio St. 2d 45, 1969) not to be capital offenses. The supreme court held the trial courts did not have the discretion to violate the constitutional rule that dollar bail must be set for noncapital offenses.

BAIL DECISION MAKING

Having given this background, descriptive data can be used to show that multiple unweighted criteria allows a wide range of behavior within this structural discretion system. This descriptive data points out that within this wide berth of structural discretion judges choose neither to provide uniform decision making nor to meet the reformers' hopes.

This descriptive data grew out of bail setting carried out in Hamilton County, Ohio, from April 1, 1977, to March 31, 1978. The data was gathered from interviews conducted by the Greater Cincinnati Bail Project Incorporated. This nonprofit corporation interviewed each prisoner detained in central facility prior to initial hearing to gather information used by the Hamilton County Municipal Court judges to set bail.[9] The questionnaire used provided information on all ten criteria set out in Rule 46. Data presented here is based on a sample of 1,228 defendants from a population of 6,400 centrally detained and interviewed defendants. (This sample provides an accuracy level equivalent to a survey of 1,500 for a national survey.) Data collection, built on two pilot projects at the Bail Project, consisted of thirty-four variables.

We will examine the behavioral discretion of the thirteen trial judges who sat on the Hamilton County Municipal Court bench during this year to see at what rate they used release on personal recognizance. By categorizing the prisoners according to those who received dollar-free bail and those required to post cash bail, differential rates of signature release can be determined. This shows the range of behavioral discretion that existed in comparison to the projection of the Vera reformers.

Defendants also can be categorized according to charge subgroups. First-misdemeanant and felony subgroups are examined to note the impact of charge on differential release-on-recognizance rates. Further subdivision of the population into violent and nonviolent charge subgroups enables comparison of how that dimension affected each judge's determination of dollar-free release.

In comparing release on signature to cash bail, we find that for none of thirteen judges did release on recognizance become the norm. Figure 4.1 shows the highest rate of release on recognizance is that of Judge A: 43 percent of the defendants, leaving 57 percent to cash bail. The range of recognizance release rates is quite wide, however, running from a low of 18 percent to a high of 43 percent. There appear to be three blocs of judges when all defendants are grouped together: (1) Judges A and B—40 percent or greater recognizance release rate; (2) Judges C, D, E, F, G, H, J, I—28-35 percent recognizance release rate; and (3) Judges K, L, M—18-22 percent recognizance release rate.

As this data shows, the judges continue to use cash bond predominantly. Local discretion has resulted in the Vera reforms being discounted for the most part. This finding has been reinforced through interviews with a number of judges. Secondly, a wide range of behavioral variation exists among the thirteen judges. This behavioral variation is, of course, consistent with discretion given to local trial court judges.

To consider the impact of charge on release rates, the prisoners are divided into misdemeanant and felony categories. Figure 4.2 shows that even among misdemeanant defendants, recognizance release is the norm or mode for only two of thirteen judges (Judges A and B). The median release on recognizance rate hovers around the 40 percent mark.

The range of recognizance release for misdemeanant defendants is considerable, running from a low of 15 percent to a high of 56 percent. The trial court judges using their discretion in reference to the ten criteria become more sharply

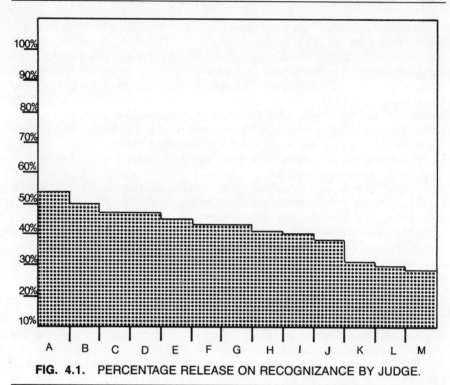

FIG. 4.1. PERCENTAGE RELEASE ON RECOGNIZANCE BY JUDGE.

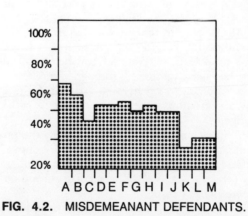

FIG. 4.2. MISDEMEANANT DEFENDANTS.

divided into the three blocs noted before: (1) A and B; (2) C, D, E, F, G, H, I, and J; and (3) K, L, and M.

Figure 4.3 illustrates the judges are closer to agreement when they set bond on felony cases. Whereas release-on-recognizance rates for misdemeanants varied by forty-one percentage points, the rates for felons varied by only twenty-two percentage points. The median recognizance release rate is 25 percent. In dashing the expectations of bail reformers that recognizance release would become the norm, the judges are close to a consensus that dollar-free signature release will be the exception and not the rule for felony defendants.

If the defendants are divided into yet smaller subgroups based on whether the charge is violent or nonviolent, we find in Figure 4.4 only two judges (A and B) are willing to free a majority of nonviolent misdemeanant defendants on their signature alone. The median signature release is 38 percent, far below the expectations of the Vera reformers. Using their discretion, the trial judges have implemented a release rate below Hartman's projection even for those defendants charged with nonviolent misdemeanors.

The range of dollar-free release for initially arraigned defendants with nonviolent misdemeanor charges runs from a low of 14 percent to a high of 55 percent—a range of 41 percent. Dollar-free release depends on the discretion of the individual judge, and significant differences exist among the judges in the way they apply the wide latitude of discretion they are given to nonviolent misdemeanant defendants.

As Figure 4.5 shows, the range in reference to dollar-free release widens for defendants with violent misdemeanors from a low of zero to a high of 60 percent. Discretion encompasses a wide area when one judge releases three out of every five defendants without charge and another releases no defendants charged with violent misdemeanors free of cost. The median release rate for detainees with violent misdemeanor charges drops to 29 percent, far below the norm hoped for by the Vera reformers. As the majority of judges pointed out in interviews, the

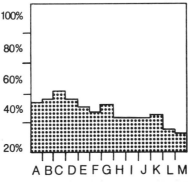

FIG. 4.3. FELONY DEFENDANTS.

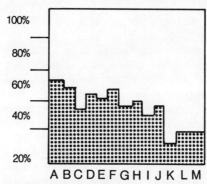

FIG. 4.4. NONVIOLENT MISDEMEANANT DEFENDANTS.

protection of the community from defendants prone to violence is a major consideration in bail setting. Being charged with a violent misdemeanor thus reduces the
probability of dollar-free release.

If we compare Figure 4.6 and Figure 4.7, we find that release rates range from
14–53 percent for nonviolent felony defendants, in contrast to a range of 0–39
percent for violent felony detainees. The range is the same — 39 percent — pointing
out the continuing behavioral differences among the judges that local trial court
discretion encourages. However, the dollar-free release rates are significantly lower
for those charged with violent felonies, as is consistent with the principle of
community safety. The median dollar-free release rate for the judges reflects this
concern. It drops from 35 percent for nonviolent felony defendants to 14 percent
for violent felony detainees. Seriousness of and the atrocity of the charge are two
key criteria for the trial court judges, outweighing the factors the bail reformers
introduced in the hopes of increasing the number freed without cost and lengthy
procedure.

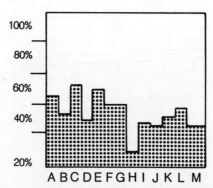

FIG. 4.5. VIOLENT MISDEMEANANT DEFENDANTS.

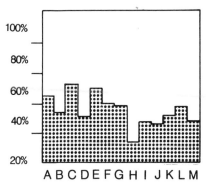

FIG. 4.6. NONVIOLENT FELONY DEFENDANTS.

CASH RELEASE

Analyzing discretionary bail decisions by dicotomizing releases into recognizance and cash bail tells us something about the reality of bail decision making: the implementation of Rule 46 is falling short of reformers' hopes. This should have been considered likely even by the reformers, given the construct of the American federal system and the wide discretion that both the ten criteria of Rule 46 and Ohio case law permits.

Another interesting issue is what the typical defendant pays for cash release, given cash release is the predominant mode. Here again a comparison of the thirteen judges is in order. An examination of all defendants together (Table 4.1) shows the most striking characteristic of this comparison is the range of median dollar bail, running from a low of $87 for Judge A to a high of $1,275 for Judge K. There seem to be four plateaus in median dollar bail: (1) A—$87; (2) B, D, E, G—$250-$286; (3) C, H, I, J—$349-$564; and (4) L, K, M—$732-$1275.

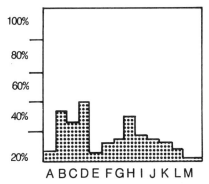

FIG. 4.7. VIOLENT FELONY DEFENDANTS.

Table 4.1.   Median dollar bails as set by thirteen Ohio judges

Judge	A	B	C	D	E	F	G	H	I	J	K	L	M
All defendants ($)	87	250	564	286	286	350	253	349	462	468	1275	732	884
Misdemeanants	0	0	380	73	41	37	69	57	50	100	83	301	81
Nonviolent	0	0	419	63	33	13	68	65	60	87	94	301	61
Violent	0	0	87	87	75	100	75	25	38	368	75	75	184
Felons	555	882	804	750	1482	1631	735	1800	1721	747	3107	1010	3207
Nonviolent	133	709	9	792	0	400	388	1667	750	583	1503	1330	605
Violent	2299	3100	2000	991	3250	2695	2231	1444	2423	912	3389	3064	3344

If defendants are divided into misdemeanant and felony subgroups, we find significantly lower bail being set for those charged with misdemeanors. The range for misdemeanors runs from $0 to $380. The data shows the two most lenient judges grant dollar-free bail, while the two most strict judges impose bail amounts greater than $300 on their "median" prisoner. Again it is clear that the discretion granted to local trial court judges results in a widely varying pattern of bail setting.

For felony defendants, the range of median dollar bail runs from $555 to $3,107. Every single judge imposes significantly higher median dollar bail for felonies in comparison to misdemeanors. This is one criterion all judges seem to utilize; as such it makes sense because it is a basic distinction in criminal law, was sanctified by previous statute and case law, and is present in Rule 46 as one of the ten criteria. There seem to be three plateaus in median felon bail: (1) A, B, C, D, G, and J—$555-$882; (2) E, F, H, I, L—$1000-$1800; and (3) K and M—$3027-$3107. Obviously, local trial court discretion led to tremendous variation in the amount of bail required for the release of felony defendants.

Again, further subdivision can be made of the prisoners into four charge groups: (1) nonviolent misdemeanor, (2) violent misdemeanors, (3) nonviolent felony, and (4) violent felony. A comparison of misdemeanors in Table 4.1 shows the range of median dollar bails for violent misdemeanors, $0-$368 is less than that for nonviolent misdemeanors, $0-$419. Beyond this, nearly as many judges set median prisoner bail lower for violent misdemeanor than nonviolent misdemeanor charges as the number who set it higher for violent misdemeanors. The remaining two judges release their "median" prisoner free of bail regardless of the violent/nonviolent aspect of the misdemeanor charge.

In cases involving felony charges, the judges exercise more of a common approach. Every judge but Judge H of the thirteen imposed significantly higher bail for violent felonies than for nonviolent felonies. The range for the "median" defendant with nonviolent felony charges ran from $0 to $1,667. In comparison, the range for median defendants with violent felony charges ran from $912 to $3,389.

For the median nonviolent defendant, five of the thirteen judges set bail under $500; five set it between $500 and $1,000; and three set it over $1,000. For the median violent felon, two of thirteen set bail between $500 and $1,000; one judge set it between $1,000 and $2,000; five set it between $2,000 and $3,000; and the highest five set bail at over $3,000. The violent dimension of a charge, therefore, makes a difference when combined with a felony charge. Local trial court discretion results in high bail being set for those with violent felony charges. As one judge pointed out in an interview, a bail of $3,000 will keep most defendants off the streets. Five of the thirteen local trial court judges were setting bail at a dollar value that makes releases unlikely for prisoners charged with a violent felony.

In conclusion, the hopes and expectations of bail reform advocates have not been fulfilled in the implementation of Rule 46. The structural discretion operationalized by the ten criteria cited in Rule 46 and, still in use in 1984, are sufficiently broad to allow local trial court judges use of their own judgement, their own discretion. The data shows cash bail the norm, not release on recognizance. Only two judges of the thirteen used recognizance release for a majority of their misdemeanant defendants.

The thirteen judges vary widely in their bail setting practice. The range of low to high bail was often quite wide. Rule 46, because of its multiple unweighted criteria, permits a wide area of discretion in bail setting in accord with Ohio tradition and case law. The federal system, Ohio tradition, and Ohio case law constituted a system in which the judges had been trained. It was this system, this ethos, and the mechanism of wide zones of discretionary power that thwarted the bail reform proposal.

CHAPTER FIVE

The Prosecutor's Discretion: Out of the Closet, Not Out of Control

SIDNEY I. LEZAK and MAUREEN LEONARD

PROSECUTORIAL DISCRETION is the power of the prosecutor to enforce the laws selectively. It begins with the decision to initiate or decline prosecution and extends through sentencing. In the selection of offenders and offenses the power of the prosecutor is almost unlimited.

Discretion is generally recognized to possess both hazards and values. It is criticized for its potential for abuse and praised for the unique and essential functions it serves in the administration of justice. The prosecutor's exercise of discretion has come under increased examination in recent years. Many commentators have called for new limitations on this overly expansive, largely unreviewed discretionary power.

That discretion possesses both positive and negative features makes suggestions for reform difficult. In the search for clearly defined parameters within which discretion might operate, one must address both "the need in prosecutorial decision-making for certainty, consistency, and an absence of arbitrariness on the one hand, and the need for flexibility, sensitivity, and adaptability on the other."[1] This chapter examines the reasons for discretion, reviews how discretion operates, and suggests an approach to the regulation of discretion. A tailored approach to the control of prosecutive discretion will most effectively confine the potential for abuse while allowing the necessary and valuable exercise of discretion in a principled fashion.

WHY DISCRETION EXISTS

The origin of our reliance on and acceptance of prosecutorial discretion is unknown. Davis identifies its development as having resulted from "unplanned drift over nearly two centuries."[2] Vorenberg suggests that the reliance on discretion is "in part a carryover from times when there was a greater sense of shared values

Sidney I. Lezak, attorney, was for twenty years the U.S. attorney in Portland, Oregon.
Maureen Leonard, attorney and formerly law clerk to U.S. Attorney Sidney I. Lezak, is currently a law clerk for Justice Betty Roberts at the Oregon Supreme Court.

about crime and criminal administration."[3] Whatever its origin, discretion now pervades all facets of justice administration. The rare, often unsuccessful challenges to its exercise serve to highlight its entrenchment.[4]

The present-day reasons for the continued existence of discretion are many. First, overcriminalization in the criminal code necessitates it. When legislatures undertake the legislation of morals, laws are often passed that reflect the ideals of the community rather than a realistic expectation of conformity. Thurman Arnold states: "Most unenforced criminal laws survive in order to satisfy moral objections to established modes of conduct. They are unenforced because we want to continue our conduct, and unrepealed because we want to preserve our morals."[5] The Mann Act, Sunday closing laws, gambling, and minor drug violations are examples of unenforced lesislative attempts to regulate morals. Enforcement of such laws often is given low priority by prosecutors because these offenses are minor and appear to pose little immediate threat to the physical well-being of the community. This approach to the criminal law—that laws should reflect the ideal rather than the necessary—may foster a reluctance to repeal antiquated laws and result in continued reliance on the prosecutor's discretion to maintain a sense of realism in the enforcement of laws.

Overcriminalization continues when legislatures too readily address perceived social ills by means of criminal sanctions, even when such sanctions provide ineffective solutions. As a result, "noncriminal" activity is dealt with through the criminal justice system, where the problem cannot be addressed and is often exacerbated. The use of penal sanctions in response to alcohol abuse provides an example. In such a case, the inappropriateness of the sanction may well lead prosecutors to forgo prosecution.

Second, even if full enforcement of existing laws were mandated, present resources would not permit compliance. The criminal code proscribes such a breadth of conduct that full enforcement is an economic impossibility. The Reagan administration's proposals for a massive prison building program in which construction costs are expected to reach two billion dollars underscores the economic realities of full enforcement.[6] Even in Germany, where the prosecutor's exercise of discretion is quite restricted by statue, discretion is expanding in response to a rising crime rate and corresponding court backlog. Germany has amended its Code of Criminal Procedure to broaden the scope of prosecutorial discretion in certain misdemeanor cases. One commentator suggests the breakdown of the compulsory prosecution principle in Germany is not far away.[7]

Third, the severity of criminal sanctions in the United States might spur the exercise of prosecutorial discretion. An examination of the West German penal code discloses that criminal sanctions are considerably harsher in the United States than in Germany. Many acts classified as felonies in the United States are misdemeanors under German code. These include larceny, embezzlement, fraud, extortion, forgery, negligent homicide, inflicting bodily harm with a weapon, and dangerous driving. German sentencing policy relies primarily on fines rather than imprisonment. As a result, between the years 1963 and 1976, although Germany experienced a rising crime rate, the national prison population markedly decreased.[8] Where imprisonment is imposed the mandatory minimum sentences are more lenient than U.S. sentences. This more lenient sentencing policy permeates Europe. It has been suggested that where a one-year sentence would be imposed in the United States, a one-month sentence would be imposed in Europe for comparable crimes.

That the United States resorts to imprisonment to a degree that far exceeds most other countries is borne out by figures that rank the United States third in the world in prisoners per capita, behind the Soviet Union and the Union of South Africa.[9] These sobering statistics document a trend that continues, a legislative response to perceived growth in crime that stacks sanction upon sanction in an attempt to "get tough" on criminals. Habitual offender statutes and lengthened mandatory minimum sentences are a few examples.

The impact of harsh sanctions on prosecutorial discretion is not well documented but may be significant. One study indicates that prosecutors will more likely exercise discretion through bargaining or dismisal if they perceive the sanctions to be inappropriate.[10] An excessive sanction might be a contributing factor to perceived inappropriateness.

Fourth, prosecutors want to win.[11] Winning is important not only for the ego satisfaction and enhancement of reputations that victory brings, but also because a record of winning makes it easier to dispose of cases by favorable plea bargains in the future. As an additional bonus, a high conviction rate makes it less likely that trials will result against defendants who, bolstered by the prosecutor's weak record of victories, might avoid plea-bargaining options in favor of the "gamble" of a trial. Such considerations may result in failure to prosecute or favorable plea bargains for serious and even heinous offenses where the prosecutor has less than supreme confidence about the result.

Fifth, law enforcement considerations support continued prosecutorial discretion. Obtaining information about other crimes or other criminals, and the difficulty of proving the crime at trial, often play a part in decisions to grant immunity or reduce charges.

Sixth, the pressure of public opinion is a "wild card" factor that is most difficult to evaluate. It is clear, however, to the extent that there is aggressive coverage by news media or oversight of specific criminal proceedings by special interest groups, that public opinion assumes an increasingly important position in the prosecutor's decisional matrix. An interesting example is the change in prosecutive policies that appeared with respect to draft evaders and protesters as the Vietnam War became increasingly unpopular. Cases that might have been prosecuted readily while the war had the support of the general public and press were screened with increasing intensity as public distaste was followed by judicial leniency. In Oregon, for example, prison sentences for draft evaders were almost universally abrogated in favor of a six-month term at a state forest camp, where environmental work was the primary task.

These reasons for discretion—overcriminalization, inadequate resources for full enforcement, harsh sanctions, the prosecutor's desire to win, law enforcement considerations, and public opinion—contribute in varying degrees to the breadth of discretion that presently exists in the criminal justice system. It is unlikely that many of these factors will be eliminated in the near future. In fact, the trends toward overcriminalization, diminishing resources, and harsh sanctions appear to be accelerating.[12] Without the elimination of some of these factors, continued discretion in the prosecutor's decision making is inevitable.

THE OPERATION OF PROSECUTIVE DISCRETION

The influence of the prosecutor's discretion is pervasive in all stages of the criminal justice system. In federal prosecutions, the decision to arrest is made by the prosecutor. In state prosecutions, this is usually the officer's decision, often tempered by his or her knowledge of the prosecutor's charging policies. The prosecutor makes sentencing recommendations to the judge following conviction. In their post-sentence reports, the prosecutors may even influence parole decisions by urging leniency for those who have cooperated or by castigating those who have not.

A recent study on actual discretionary practices by prosecutors' offices has isolated two important influences on the charging decision: (1) office policy and (2) the manner of review of the initial charging decision.[13] According to the authors, four office policies appear to underlie the manner in which prosecutorial discretion is exercised in the decision to charge. The first policy is termed *legal sufficiency*, a porous filtering process at the intake stage of the criminal justice system. At the time of his or her initial contact with a case, the prosecutor forwards for further consideration all those in which the investigative report indicates there is a "legally sufficient" case. Weeding out cases is done at the second level of review in those offices that use such a policy.

A second policy, *system efficiency*, has as its primary goal the retention of "organization control, efficient management, and accountability" in its decisional process. The office the authors describe as most conscientiously engaged in such a policy is the Kings County (Brooklyn) New York District Attorney's Office, which processes more than eighty thousand felony and misdemeanor arrests each year. The system handles this volume through a highly mechanistic classification of cases that produces an enormous percentage of dismissals. By the appointment of the Early Case Assessment Bureau, the Kings County office initiated procedures to prevent overcharging. "Under this policy the prosecutor continuously explores additional avenues for case dispositions, examines cases for their plea bargaining potential and extensively uses community resources, especially treatment and diversion programs."[14]

A third policy focuses on *defendant rehabilitation*. This policy, which has been accepted in the rather special environment of Boulder County, Colorado, relies on noncriminal justice system resources and community support to assist in moving eligible defendants out of the criminal justice system. This liberal diversion policy is accompanied by the express policy of increased toughness on those offenders remaining in the system. This conservatism was viewed, in part, as a response to community concerns about a potential lack of accountability in the criminal justice system.

A final policy, *trial sufficiency*, focuses on making a charge in the initial system encounter with which the prosecutor expects to stick through trial. This calls for a maximum amount of accurate information from the investigative agencies and early consideration of alternatives to prosecution.

The existence of a review process for initial charging decisions also has an influence on the exercise of discretion. In some offices, individual attorneys appear to make the charging decision and handle the case through initial appearances, grand jury, and trial, with little formal review. In other offices, there are more formalized units with experienced supervisory attorneys playing an active role in monitoring the charging decision. Of course, with respect to those cases ultimately reaching trial, there is a review of the decision by the court, and prosecutors are likely to hear quickly of trial judges' criticisms of the charging decision.

Most prosecutors' offices have some organization, either formal or informal, for the screening of cases. An increasing number of offices, under the urging of the National District Attorneys Association for local prosecutors and the Department of Justice for federal prosecutors, U.S. attorneys have or are establishing written guidelines in an effort to reduce disparities resulting from unbridled individual discretion.

The Oregon U.S. Attorney's Office, for instance, during the authors' tenure separated the initial intake function from the ultimate charging decision. Each case, with the exception of petty offenses, was filtered through a rotating assignment committee of experienced criminal assistants after the attorney on the Criminal Intake Desk (also a rotating job) made the initial decision to accept the case. The assignment committee then had an opportunity to take a second look at the case at a time when more information usually was available and could overrule or approve the initial decision to charge. Questions of policy were expected to be identified by the attorneys at every level and taken up with the U.S. attorney or his designate.

Written guidelines for the Oregon U.S. Attorney's office, in addition to the general principles of federal prosecution promulgated by the Department of Justice in Washington, D.C., are available to provide a starting point for this discretionary decision making.

Review of the initial charging decision also might be appropriate in the occasional case where an investigative agency feels aggrieved because prosecution has been declined. The relatively small number of persons involved in the agencies dealing regularly with an office of this kind makes it possible to accommodate such review.

TOWARD A LIMIT ON DISCRETION
The Dissatisfaction with Discretion. Concerns with the use and abuse of prosecutorial discretion are well taken, for nothing is as potentially destructive of a community sense of well-being as the arbitrary enforcement of the laws. Davis writes that the present degree of prosecutorial discretion is excessive. "The vast quantities of unnecessary discretionary power that have grown up in our system should be cut back and the discretionary power that is found to be necessary should be properly confined, structured, and checked."[15] Givelber writes that abuse of prosecutorial discretion can jeopardize important societal values, frustrate

the will of the legislature and the citizenry, make a mockery of the principle of fair notice, and create the appearance of a fundamentally unfair and arbitrary government.[16] Arzt, comparing compulsory with discretionary prosecution, states that the latter distorts sanctions, undermines the purpose of the substantive law, and possesses superior repressive capacity.[17] Underlying such criticisms is the recognition that a system of selective enforcement by unscrupulous prosecutors can turn the criminal code into a tool of harassment and repression of select members of the community. The decision not to prosecute — for Davis, a negative decision — may be made for equally improper motives. These "invisible" acts of discretion are particularly elusive of review.

Vorenberg has considered effects on the justice system of excessive reliance on discretion:

> Excessive reliance on discretion has a deeper effect. It hides malfunctions in the criminal justice system and avoids difficult policy judgments by giving the appearance that they do not have to be made. It obscures the need for additional resources and makes misapplication of available resources more likely. And it promotes a pretense that we know more than we do, thereby leading to wrong decisions and preempting research and evaluation on which change should be based. Discretionary decisionmaking has helped keep cases moving through the system without too many embarrassing questions, while promoting the sense that compassion and wisdom are at work. The result has been some compassion (often matched or exceeded by unfairness) and very little wisdom.[18]

Central to the above-noted concerns is the recognition that discretion can operate as an impediment to needed change. By obscuring the need for hard policy decisions regarding such issues as the allocation of resources, punishment theories, treatment of prisoners, and standards for bail, excessive discretion can stifle attempts to improve the criminal justice system.

The Benefits of Discretion. Discretion fulfills valuable functions otherwise unobtainable in the administration of justice. A decision not to charge a suspect may serve to preserve the presumption of innocence. It is appropriate that the prosecutor screen out cases in which the evidence is weak or the witnesses lack credibility. The hardships of trial should not be inflicted on defendants whose guilt the prosecutor finds highly questionable.

Discretion also is an indispensible source of individualization in the administration of justice. Because it would be impossible for a legislative body to address all the situations in which a law might apply, laws are necessarily written in general language with application to the majority. Yet we pride ourselves on a system of individualized justice. We recognize that a mechanistic application of the law can be inadequate and frequently unjust.[19] We expect that the circumstances of each case will be evaluated individually so that punishment is tailored to culpability. "To the extent that dissimilarities between offenders have significance from an ethical and moral, as well as a practical and administrative, point of view, they lend an idealistic basis for the selection process."[20] The prosecutor's decision appropriately encompasses an evaluation of all the circumstances of the crime, including its severity, the accused's criminal record, and mitigating factors. Decisions to forgo prosecution in certain circumstances serve the interests of justice.

Further, discretion allows for creativity in the system. To the extent that a rigid application of the law is not always successful, discretion accommodates creative alternatives. Discretion also serves law enforcement purposes by allowing prosecutors room within which to bargain for information or testimony essential for convictions. Finally, discretion is efficient in that it provides a degree of necessary finality to decisions made within discretionary powers.

Given that the utilization of prosecutorial discretion results in both benefits and detriments to the administration of justice, the question obviously becomes how best to regulate its exercise to maximize its benefits and minimize its abuse. Reforms that call for the elimination of all discretion go too far. A blanket revision to a system of compulsory prosecution, when practicalities permit only selective enforcement, would drive discretion underground and stifle attempts to control and channel its use.

Suggested reforms that would cut back discretion through the elimination of some of the reasons for its existence illustrate one sensible approach to limiting discretion. However, trends in criminal justice administration indicate that change in these areas probably will not be soon forthcoming.

Of greater use are reforms that present some middle ground. Such an approach would begin with a recognition that, while elimination of all discretion is impossible and probably undesirable, and while large quantities of discretion probably will remain in the system, effective checks can be placed on the exercise of discretion through existing control mechanisms. Such an approach should begin with an attempt to match specific problem areas in the exercise of discretion with those mechanisms of control best suited for limiting and channeling discretion.

An overview of the writing in the area of prosecutorial discretion reveals that concerns regarding the abuse of discretion appear to have two principal components: individual conduct and system uniformity. The first component, individual prosecutorial conduct, arises when a prosecutor uses the office to engage in harrassment, repression, retaliation, or favoritism. The prosecutor's conduct is improper either because it violates individual liberties, such as freedom of speech or association, or because motives beyond those of law enforcement influence the charging decision.

The second component is a concern for system uniformity.[21] It is illustrated when two prosecutors in the same office, exercising their discretion with proper motives and within the permissible bonds of prosecutorial discretion, reach differing dispositions of similar cases. The defendant with the least satisfactory (to him or her) disposition may have suffered no constitutional violation or improperly motivated prosecution. And yet the "presumption of regularity" in the administration of justice has not been met. This system uniformity component is premised upon the recognition that the aggregate of prosecutive decisions, both officewide and over time, should reveal a cohesive, rather than formless, application of the laws.

Controls on the exercise of discretion may be imposed by the legislature, the judiciary, or the executive at state or federal levels. The avenues available to each of the three branches of government are well known. The legislature allocates resources and drafts legislation. Either activity can have potentially far-reaching impact upon the exercise of prosecutorial discretion.[22] The judiciary reviews instances of challenged prosecutorial discretion and in a case-by-case adjudication sets standards by which a prosecutor's actions may be judged. The executive or an agency thereof may promulgate internal guidelines and disciplinary measures for its prosecutors.

Many commentators have analyzed the efficacy of these three mechanisms in the regulation of discretion and have concluded that each has serious deficiencies. These inadequacies, however, may not be inherent in the control mechanism but may, rather, result from attempting to apply one solution to two distinct problems. As has been discussed, prosecutorial discretion involves questions of individual conduct as well as of system uniformity. To be successful, a suggested reform must attempt to address both components. This can be accomplished only by a recognition that a variety of control mechanisms is required to regulate discretion, and that a mechanism that successfully regulates individual prosecutorial conduct probably will be ineffective in controlling system uniformity. Each control mechanism must be utilized to some degree if effective limits on discretion are to come about.

The judiciary has fashioned for itself a limited role in regulating prosecutorial discretion. Until recently, courts have recognized only a few bases for challenging a prosecutor's decision, the familiar ones being class-specific treatment and decisions based on favoritism or vindictiveness. With few exceptions challenges raising concerns about whether an individual was treated consistently with others in similar circumstances have not been considered appropriate for judicial review.

Yick Wo v. Hopkins presents the traditional scope of judicial review of prosecutorial discretion. In that case, the U.S. Supreme Court recognized that the equal protection clause of the U.S. Constitution protects against unconstitutionally motivated prosecutions:

> Though the law itself be fair on its face and impartial in appearance, yet, if it is applied and administered by public authority with an evil eye and an unequal hand, so as practically to make unjust and illegal discriminations between persons in similar circumstances, material to their rights, the denial of equal justice is still within the prohibition of the constitution.[23]

A recent application of this judicial rule is found in *Murguia v. Municipal Court*.[24] The issue arose on an appeal from a denial of defendants' request for a discovery order. Defendants attempted to compel the prosecutor to turn over evidence to support their claim of discriminatory law enforcement against members of the United Farm Workers Union. The issue, as the court phrased it, was whether the prosecution is constitutionally free to select only these defendants and prosecute them only because they are members of a certain class, the union. The court stated that "the principal objective of the equal protection guarantee with respect to administrative enforcement of statutes is to safeguard individuals from administrative officials who utilize their discretionary powers of selective enforcement as a vehicle for intentional invidious discrimination." The court found defendants' allegations of an intentional, purposeful selective enforcement policy directed against members and supporters of the UFW sufficient to justify granting their discovery motion. The court also indicated that should defendants succeed in proving the claimed discrimination, such a policy of selective enforcement would be a defense to prosecution. The concurring opinion cautions that the defense of discriminatory prosecution should be available to those very limited number of persons "who can establish that they could not otherwise have been prosecuted but for 'such discriminatory conduct.'"

Judicial reluctance to approach the broader issues underlying the pursuit of consistency in the enforcement of laws may reflect, in part, the perceived limited efficacy of the trial, and hence judicial review, as a decision-making technique. Cramton argues that the trial is most effective when used to resolve specific issues of fact between a limited number of parties. He asserts: "The focus on 'justice in the individual case' does not lend itself to intelligent forward planning, to a rational consideration of major options and alternatives, and to a concern for the aggregate effects of individualized decisions."[25]

Under this analysis, judicial review proves a less satisfactory tool for the regulation of system uniformity. The goal of equal distribution of justice can be achieved only when the application of principled criteria to the myriad of factual circumstances results in relatively consistent charging decisions. The method of regulation necessary to achieve this consistency must be proscriptive in focus and capable of synthesizing a wide range of variables. It also must be capable of accommodating a "concern for the aggregate effects of individualized decisions."

Abrams reaches a similar conclusion concerning this apparent inadequacy of judicial review. He states: "The unevenness of application inherent in a multiple decision-maker system operating without articulated criteria is of great concern. And judicial review is not well adapted to correctly such unevenness."[26]

Legislatures can play an important role in the regulation of system uniformity. Policymaking concerning such issues as prosecution priorities and the allocation of resources in the prosecutor's office are most appropriately made in the legislative forum, where visibility and responsiveness to the citizenry are key elements. Vorenberg suggests that policymaking should come from the legislators, not from individual prosecutors, and where legislation will not work prosecutors should be given the authority to exercise discretion openly, through "conscious legislative decision rather than a process of arrogation or default."[27] While legislative controls possess only limited utility in the direct regulation of discretion, legislatures can appropriately and effectively direct the issuance of guidelines and review procedures and can appropriate the funds necessary for compliance.

The direct regulation of system uniformity is best accomplished through internal guidelines established by the executive branch or delegated to supervisory prosecutors. Guidelines initiated internally, rather than imposed from the outside, appear to have a better chance of acceptance and thus success. In addition, guidelines can be drawn with specificity yet avoid the rigidity of legislation, which is binding law. The recognition of a "lack of generally shared values about the goals of criminal administration"[28] among prosecutors themselves makes guidelines imperative. The Department of Justice Principles of Federal Prosecution provide a model.

A requirement of written reasons for the disposition of cases and a system of periodic review for compliance and consistency would substantially increase the effectiveness of guidelines. The importance of publication of guidelines should not be underestimated. Suspicions of improper influences, ad hoc decision making, and behind-the-scenes dealings in the prosecutor's office are not uncommon. Improprieties rarely occur, but their existence is widely assumed by an increasingly cynical public. Indeed, Vorenberg alludes to the erosion of trust in criminal justice administration as one of the contributing factors to the growing concern with prosecutorial discretion. The increased consciousness of the exercise of bias on the basis of race, sex, creed, or ethnic origin is a similar factor. These factors create special needs for notice and visibility in any reforms attempted in the area of prosecutorial discretion.

Open office communication and the involvement of more than one prosecutor in the charging decision will facilitate uniformity. While internal guidelines cannot guarantee a uniform application of the laws, they provide meaningful and effective parameters within which prosecutors can operate.

CHAPTER   SIX

Discretion and Judicial Sentencing

CARL F. PINKELE

PERHAPS no area of the law system commands more attention with respect to questions about discretion than that of judicial behavior. One need only take the most casual of glances at the behavior of judges—from the U.S. Supreme Court to local justices of the peace and magistrates—to sense fully that authority at these points in the law system is extensively discretionary in kind.

The reality of wide latitude and flexibility in judicial policymaking raises critical issues for any democratic polity. What does it mean for a system supposedly governed by rules for the people to in fact have public policies made by virtually autonomous individuals? How can a theoretically democratic system be squared with a reality in which judges, on the basis of their own viewpoints, can establish policies?

This chapter considers the general environment that encourages judicial discretion within the law system, turns to a brief case study of judicial discretion in practice, and makes some observations about it within the context of a democratic polis.

For some time a debate has taken place among those who would address these issues quite differently indeed. One pattern of answers, often but not exclusively associated today with the contemporary neoconservative attack upon judicial activism, is to by and large decry it. The neoconservative position importunes us to find in judicial policymaking a wide variety of ills, not the least of which are forms of tyranny.[1] Answering the charges of those who decry judicial activism are others who basically combine two perspectives. Judicial interpretations, according to a judicial activism position, are impossible to avoid; therefore, to presume that a judge can avoid injecting personality or beliefs into an action flies in the face of reality. Second, because there is much more to being democratic than either considerations of simple majoritarianism or adherence to legislatively established rules—both of which are process orientations—a tribunal of review, such as courts, justices, and judges, is not in and of itself necessarily antidemocratic.[2] In this projudicial activism pattern of thought, the burden of proof falls more upon what

Carl F. Pinkele, Ohio Wesleyan University, Delaware, Ohio.

is done (the product of behavior), rather than upon how the behavior was accomplished (the process issue). Clearly our normative and descriptive perceptions are in the judicial activist camp.

There are two distinguishable judicial discretionary modes: (1) those matters in which judges have direct or explicit leverage, and (2) those in which they have an indirect discretionary influence. What follows is a brief look at the second mode and a focus on one specific aspect—sentencing behavior—of the direct/explicit form of judicial discretion.

The indirect or implicit influences upon judges arise primarily because of their pivotal location in the law system. Judicial behavior of the nonappellate variety resembles the narrow opening in an hourglass. While there are numerous ingredients in various mixes both prior to and subsequent to judicial action, everything is shaped and rearranged by passing through the judicial opening. The judicial domain in this sense indirectly influences a considerable amount of law system behavior. One often finds that prior to actual judicial action an anticipated reaction situation occurs among such actors as the police officer or the prosecutor, and the tasks of one who is to implement judicial decisions are affected by the way judges carry out their functions. That is, individuals throughout the law system in other than judicial positions will to a significant extent contour their own behavior according to what they think will occur at the judicial stage. Confronted by a "let 'um go Mo" traffic judge, for example, a patrol officer will more than likely not ticket a particular speeder; a cop on the beat who believes a local judge is particularly harsh or lenient on dope possession will act accordingly; or a person responsible for carrying out judicial decisions or decrees will attend to those tasks mindful of the degree of supervision kept by the judiciary.

The effects of indirect judicial discretion are difficult to measure precisely, or even to separate from other variables in most instances. On the other hand, explicit discretionary mechanisms available to the judiciary are numerous, recognizable, and often available for quite precise analysis. From such characteristics as subtle overt behavior within the courtroom environment itself—setting bail, instructing the jury (when there is one), and sentencing—nonappellate judicial behavior should be appropriately characterized as the almost exclusive domain of Her Honor.

There are, to be sure, institutional and structural checks upon judicial performance of both political and judicial system varieties. One immediately thinks of judicial review, although there is ample reason to believe that this can be more of a symbolic than a real check.[3] Judges might, on rare occasions, also have their decisions and practices opened for wider political investigation. Just such occurred in the rather startling contemporary case in southwestern Wisconsin in which a judge handed down a most lenient sentence to a twenty-year-old male for engaging in sexual activities with the five-year-old daughter of the woman with whom he was cohabiting. The judge in this case found the girl's behavior to be "provocative" and therefore said the male's behavior was wrong, but understandable. In this instance several people from the area brought political pressure to remove the judge for his actions. (The recall effort, however, was unsuccessful.) In the overwhelming number of instances, most judges are relatively secure against "outside" political action, as well as against judicial pressures and constraints. Even in instances where judges have to stand for election, there is little or no attention paid to a judge's behavior. The facts of incumbency, partisanship, and standing with the local bar association are far more determinative of reelection results.[4]

Judicial behavior supposedly is held in check institutionally and theoretically through the operation of judicial review. Judicial review theoretically is always there. (The classic position is that of John Marshall in *Marbury v. Madison* [1803].) It is predicated upon the noble notion that the behavior of no one in a position of authority can be excluded from another's scrutiny. It exists, furthermore, to bring otherwise disparate decisions into line and under generally applicable rules. Judicial review does not exist to make all judicial behavior result in the same policy for similar cases; however, it does help to bring about a pattern of decision making that allows for predictability and, in that sense, rationality to obtain.

Borrowing Dworkin's doughnut analogy, judicial review often delineates and demarcates the parameters of judicial behavior in particular arenas.[5] Like the doughnut, the parameters articulated through judicial review act as general constraints upon the interior process, although they do not necessarily dictate the exact nature of results therein. All manner of judicial results have constituted and shall continue to constitute "the doughnut's fillings." This is to say that the overall impact of judicial review has been an attempt to square the gross legal product (through due process mainly) with broad constitutional interpretation, not to impose one manner of decision for each substantive area of the law.

The reality is that operationally judicial behavior is rarely brought directly within the orbit of the review mechanisms. Only a small number of cases are actually appealed, although this number varies in relation to categories of cases. Few noncriminal cases are appealed, and the instances of criminal appeal cases are small in relation to the number actually tried. If cases handled through plea bargaining and guilty pleas are taken into consideration, the percentage not appealed grows considerably.

What we are confronted with is a situation within the law system wherein the behavior of judges is neither checked much nor institutionally tightly constrained. The institutional or structural mechanisms, as well as the political-cultural factors that would seem to be the parameters for guiding judicial behavior, actually operate quite loosely when they function at all. At best, existing constraints probably are viewed more often than not by judicial people as obstacles to get around rather than as beacons of legal light to be followed. What the judge does when under no constraints, how she performs her institutional policymaking function, is probably not only what will happen in any given instance but what shall remain the case. The theoretical possibilities that are extant do not, as a rule, negatively affect the autonomy of the judge as an actor within the law system.

A CASE STUDY

Results of research conducted by the author and Professor Monte Piliawsky of Dillard University can provide a picture of judicial discretion in operation. This case study is limited in time and place, but we believe it to be representative.

The New Orleans criminal courts contain ten sections, each presided over by a different judge. Two of these, I and J, were created by the state legislature during the spring session of 1969 to handle the heavy case load pressing upon the already existing eight sections of New Orleans criminal courts.

In June 1969 Governor John J. McKeithen appointed Israel M. Augustine, Jr., as judge of Section I and Alvin V. Oser as judge of Section J of the Criminal District Court for the Parish of Orleans. Both of these men were appointed to terms of office ending December 31, 1970; in 1971 Judges Augustine and Oser were elected to serve twelve-year terms on the criminal court. Mr. Augustine, incidentally, thereby became the first elected black judge on the Orleans criminal court bench.

Judge Oser at the time of his election was in his mid-forties. The son of a former judge, he attended Catholic schools in New Orleans. Upon graduation from Tulane University School of Law, he served as counsel for the Criminal Division of the Legal Aid Bureau until May 1962, when he was appointed assistant district attorney for Orleans Parish. As assistant district attorney, Oser handled prosecution of all capital cases and was adviser to the Orleans Parish Grand Jury. He held this position until he was elected to the criminal court bench in 1969.

Judge Augustine attended the city's public schools, graduated from Southern University in Baton Rouge, and received the law degree from Lincoln University of Law in St. Louis. In 1954 he ran for a position on the Orleans Parish School Board, receiving 23,000 votes in defeat, the largest number obtained to that time by a black candidate for that position since Reconstruction. In 1956 Augustine was elected second vice-president of the National Bar Association. In 1957 he helped organize the Southern Christian Leadership Conference and served as its general counsel. He opened his own law firm in 1958. Between 1958 and his appointment to the criminal court, Augustine served on the boards of numerous prestigious community organizations and committees, including the Community Relations Council, the Metropolitan Area Committee, the Human Relations Council, the Urban League of Greater New Orleans, and the Mayor's Committee on Crime and Delinquency.

In the New Orleans study, Judges Augustine and Oser were paired and disposition of criminal cases before Sections I and J during the first half of the 1976 court session was examined. The files used were arranged by docket number. A number was assigned to each case by the clerk of the Criminal District Court according to the order in which cases were brought to him. The numbering pattern appears to contain no systematic bias that might influence the disposition of cases brought before each section of the court. We have no evidence indicating that cases were channeled to either judge for any particular reason whatsoever.

The criminal district court in New Orleans hears most cases involving violations of state law. The violations range from petty crimes such as a violation of the state fishing license law, which usually draw a minimal fine, to violations involving major crimes such as robbery, theft, or narcotics.

All of the cases on the dockets of the two judges for the first half of 1976 were included in the study. All of the cases heard in Judge Augustine's court from February 20, 1976, through July 30, 1976 (N = 290), and all cases in Oser's court from March 19, 1976, through November 5, 1976 (N = 300) were analyzed. Judge Augustine handled 290 cases in 156 days—an average of 1.9 cases per calendar day—and Judge Oser took 224 days to dispose of 300 cases—an average of 1.3 cases per calendar day.

How does the judge fit into the law process? If not at the center, judges are but a short step away from it. In the New Orleans criminal justice process, the district attorney is a critical fixture. Decisions about prosecuting, the substance of the charge, and recommendations to the court upon convictions are examples of the discretionary powers of the district attorney. The district attorney is also the key ingredient in the all-important activity of plea bargaining.[6]

In most instances during the operation of the criminal justice process, there is no trial. Guilt or innocence is "determined" through bargaining prior to the actual involvement of a judge in the process. When plea bargaining occurs the role of the judge is to sentence, and generally the judge simply legitimizes plea bargaining arrangements.

When there is a trial, however, the judge becomes a significant factor at almost every turn. One feature of the New Orleans scene is significant here: the large majority of trials held are deliberations before a judge without the presence of a jury. In such a setting the judge becomes an important decision maker in the dual sense of assessing guilt (most defendants who do come to trial are convicted) and pronouncing sentence. In their own domain, judges do exercise a considerable amount of discretion with respect to what happens to those appearing before them.

In the area of convictions there is a dramatic distance between the two judges studied here. Augustine consistently was less likely to acquit a defendant than was Oser. Eliminating all of the cases in which the defendant was a fugitive, was deceased, or for other reasons did not appear, and also those in which the case was dismissed through the prosecutor's plea of nolle prosequi, it was found that Judge Augustine handled a total of 242 cases and Judge Oser disposed of 238 cases within the time of the study. There was a substantial likelihood of being found guilty in both Oser's and Augustine's courts; however, of the two, Augustine was more likely to render a guilty verdict than was Oser. Twenty-eight defendants were found to be not guilty (11.8 percent) in Judge Oser's courtroom, whereas but ten (2.4 percent) shared such a happy fate in Augustine's bailiwick.

In the respective sentencing practices and patterns of Judge Augustine and Judge Oser, the differences between them become apparent. These differences are displayed in Table 6.1.

Table 6.1. General sentencing patterns of two New Orleans criminal court judges

Prison terms	Augustine		Oser	
5 years plus	34	(14.7%)	23	(11.0%)
1–5 years	77	(33.2%)	68	(32.4%)
6 months to 1 year	39	(16.8%)	30	(14.3%)
6 months or less	82	(35.3%)	89	(42.3%)
Total	232	(100%)	210	(100%)

These data suggest that while there is an interesting rough similarity in their sentencing practices, Judge Augustine is a somewhat harsher sentencing judge than his colleague. Their differences are also reflected in Oser's higher acquittal rate and in the fact that the judges' dissimilarities are greatest at the upper and lower extremes of the scale.

Although the number of cases handled by each judge involving armed robbery was relatively small (13 and 6, excluding cases dismissed through the prosecutor's plea of nolle prosequi), the differences between the judges in sentencing is apparent. Judge Augustine handed out the following prison terms to those convicted of armed robbery (in years): 99, 65, 20, 15, 10, 6, 6, 5, 5, 5, 5, 0.7. On the other hand, Judge Oser meted out the following sentences for the same offense (in years): 20, 5, 5, 2.5, 2.5, 2.5. The judges sentenced a similar number of defendants convicted of assault and battery: Augustine 12 cases and Oser 14 cases. Augustine's sentences for this crime averaged 0.94 years, double Oser's average of 0.46 years.

There were virtually no differences between the two judges' sentencing patterns for the three less violent crimes of simple burglary, receiving stolen articles, and theft. In fact, contrary to the pattern in other situations, Judge Augustine allocated slightly shorter sentences for the latter two crimes; he also handed out shorter average sentences to those convicted of one major crime, possession of concealed weapons.

The general sentencing or allocation of penalties pattern of the two judges is dramatically reversed for the sale of narcotics. The average prison sentence levied in these instances by Judge Oser is almost three times longer than that of Judge Augustine (2.1 years compared to 0.8 years). As indicated earlier, however, Judge Oser acquitted almost twice as many defendants as did Judge Augustine. Oser, interestingly, did not place a single narcotics-related defendant on inactive probation. Augustine placed more than one-half of the narcotics-related defendants (25 out of 47) on inactive probation. If Judge Oser did not acquit a particular defendant on a narcotics charge, he was likely to sentence him to a very stiff prison sentence: twice as long on the average as that given a convicted thief and four times as long as that for a person convicted of assault and battery. For his part, Judge Augustine gave prison sentences to only 40 percent of those charged with sale of narcotics, and he sentenced those to a relatively short period of incarceration.

GOING FORWARD ON JUDICIAL DISCRETION

A case study should serve several purposes; it should either provide a sharp illustration of a general pattern or offer an example of a significant diversion from the normal or expected course. A case study also should assist in fruitful extrapolation about theoretically important questions.

This case study, limited in time and circumstance as it is, provides a clear snapshot of the general systemwide realities of judicial discretion in sentencing. The actions of the New Orleans judges reflect the prevalent discretionary norm in sentencing and the widely disparate discretionary effect of sentencing differences.

Those actions accurately and clearly reflect the fact that in matters of sentencing, judicial discretion is extensive.

What does it mean for the law system to have at its hub so powerful an institution with a wide, well-shielded discretionary orbit? What remedies are available to lessen the impact of judicial discretion? These are two of the more relevant policy and theoretical questions generated by judicial discretion for a healthy democratic polity.

The presence of differential sentencing as a result of judicial discretion also raises the fundamental question of equity or equality. It is obvious that up and down the law system individuals are treated differently when charged with, convicted of, or serving time for similar transgressions. The burden of proof in a democratic system must rest upon those in authority to provide a justification for why it is not unfair, and therefore wrong (at the procedural as well as the substantive level of concerns), for differential treatment to obtain. Chapter 1 of this volume proposes a democratic justification for differences in treatment and explores the potential of discretion in providing for a healthier democratic decision-making environment.

Beyond that, one point does need further comment. Public policymaking actors—in this case judges—should provide everyone concerned, including both defendants and citizens, with a written argument that explains discretionary actions descriptively and prescriptively. As citizens and as those immediately affected by judicial behavior, we need access to judicial rationales and reasoning in order to respond to a judge's general performance through such mechanisms as elections. Such a procedure would allow for decisions to be made and would set those decisions where they belong—in the general bailiwick of politics.[7]

As much as we would like the case to be otherwise, the reality of judicial discretion, particularly in the area of sentencing, hardly resembles anything compatible with a democratic environment. Kenneth Culp Davis refers to judicial sentencing as "one of the best examples of unstructured discretionary power."[8] Indeed, the overwhelming bulk of evidence suggests sentencing patterns that reflect class, racial, and sexual biases, hardly the stuff of a healthy democracy.

Given that true democracy is a yet unobtained goal (but not unobtainable!), some interim responses to what in effect amounts to unconstrained discretion are in order. Although they do not avoid all of the problems prevalent now in discretionary sentencing, three remedies do strike at the heart of the matter and could produce a healthier judicial decision-making climate. These three ideas are not new, yet placing the three in an overall strategy designed to create a healthier, more democratic environment may well be novel.

The first notion is to establish parameters for sentencing in similar situations. This should have to be done on a nationwide basis. There is no legitimate room for the sort of random, unrelated patchwork picture that today characterizes the state-by-state (sometimes even within state) patterns of sentencing practices. The only jurisdictional boundary that makes any sense at all is that of the nation-state (and this is debatable in areas such as human rights). By placing the scope of the sentencing issue within the broadest possible parameters, there is a real possibility of canceling the sort of parochial pressures that have led repeatedly to some of the most flagrant violations of justice.

Another partial remedy would be the concurrent tightening of judicial review operations and expansion of their scope. While judicial review institutionally does exist and does sometimes operate to check sentencing behavior, for the most part it is not all that consequential. Two features would serve to make a judicial review mechanism attractive as a counterweight to the loosely attended autonomy judges have today: (1) that judges be required to submit written reasons for the sentence selected or constructed; and (2) that at various steps up the line in the judicial system (for instance, at the level of the state supreme courts) a separate ombudsman operation could function as a clearinghouse for individual sentencing decisions. Such a supervisory position would have as its primary duties checking for any violations of the principle of impartiality and publicizing the reasonings behind judicial sentencing practices.[9]

Finally, and of greatest importance, it is fundamentally critical to set judicial sentencing within a political perspective. There is no better example anywhere than judicial sentencing of what are essentially political activities—who gets what, when, and how. We must take the time and energies (no doubt it will require considerable amounts of both) to pull, twist, and turn our collective way toward wrestling with what sort of society it is that we want, or should want in order to be democratic.

At minimum, if we want to be a democratic society, we shall want judges as well as other public figures of authority in sentencing to act not for their own narrow purposes or to vent a particular bias or prejudice. These privately orchestrated actions are incompatible with the purposes of and behavior within a democratic system. Such purposes do not necessarily dictate that sentencing be of a particular variety, although limits must exist to avoid both vengeance and cruel and unusual punishment. What does count is that the reasons behind discretionary judicial decisions be sound and open to direct and indirect citizen review.

CHAPTER SEVEN

Discretion in the Sentencing and Parole Processes

DAVID   KALINICH

THE RECENT TREND in the criminal justice system is to attempt to control the discretionary powers of judges, parole boards, and their respective servants, probation and parole officers.[1] It is popular to talk about disparate sentencing, parole decision making, and the emotional impact inequitable sentencing has on the offender who is sentenced "unfairly." In Michigan it is popular to discuss how "unfair" it is that a Detroit resident must be convicted of auto theft on several occasions before he is sentenced to prison, while a first offender in a small town in the Upper Peninsula will go directly to prison. Disparate sentencing also takes place within the same jurisdiction. There exists a community in southern Ohio where one judge would grant probation to offenders convicted of marijuana sales while his colleague, whose courtroom was some thirty yards away, would sentence a similar offender to twenty to forty years in the Ohio penal system.

Disparity in sentencing goes deeper than official judicial decisions in that judges get most of the information on convicted offenders from their probation officers. Probation officers may have differing values, and they may present the information with differing emphasis and/or interpret the information differently, submitting different recommendations on similar cases.[2]

Similar criticisms have been made about the parole decision-making process in that parole board members probably have personal idiosyncrasies that affect decision making.[3] A parole board member I knew had a rigid attitude toward offenders who committed felonies while carrying a gun, while his colleagues took a more flexible or holistic view of the inmate. Similar to the sentencing process, parole board members get information on offenders' past histories from presentence investigations, when available, and institutional conduct and progress reports from a myriad of professional and custodial personnel in the institutions, compounding the chances of inequitable parole decision making.

It also is argued that there is probably a great deal of disparity in probation

David Kalinich, Michigan State University, East Lansing.

and parole revocation, even though probationers and parolees are guaranteed due process before their freedom can be taken away.[4]

The disparities that appear in the sentencing and parole process are created by individual differences and idiosyncrasies of the decision makers, as well as the information gatherers, in the criminal justice system as they apply their legitimate professional discretion. The disparities in the process traditionally have been rationalized as equitable because professionals were making decisions that somehow related to the rehabilitation or rehabilitation potential of the offender. However, the recent collapse of confidence in the system's ability to rehabilitate offenders or predict their future behavior has effectively eliminated that traditional rationalization. Disparate sentencing and parole decision making are now considered capricious and inequitable, not purposeful. Thus steps are being taken to limit the discretion of criminal-justice practitioners who make sentencing and parole decisions or who significantly affect the decision-making process.[5]

The thesis of this chapter is that attempts to limit practitioners' discretion in this arena will change the focus of decision making or drive the application of discretion underground. This notion is derived from basic organizational behavior theory and from personal experience as a practitioner in adult probation and parole work.

CURRENT APPROACHES TO LIMITING DISCRETION

In response to changing attitudes, some states have moved to a "flat sentencing" procedure that attempts to eliminate judicial discretion. Sentences are fixed by statute and, ideally, they relate to the crime. The offender's background and personal details are not considered.

A variation of the flat sentence allows for some decision making based on the intent of the offender, the seriousness of the offense, and/or the previous criminal record. For example, crimes may be classified by degrees, such as first-degree burglary, second-degree burglary, and third-degree burglary. An amateur who on a lark breaks into a grocery store thus may receive a flat sentence different from that of a professional criminal who very calculatingly breaks into a home with the intent of making a profit. No one would argue these are not the types of considerations that the average judge in his probation department should consider when sentencing individuals. However, the argument is made that by legislating these decisions in advance of sentencing, sentencing then will be equal within the state jurisdiction.

In response to new attitudes toward the parole process, parole has been eliminated in Indiana and watered down considerably in California, where a complex sentencing process has been established. The federal system has gone voluntarily to a structured form of parole decision making that presumably makes the process objective and potentially equitable. Several states are considering similar controls over their parole systems.

Limits also have been placed on probation and parole officers and prison personnel who provide information to the judges and paroling authorities involved in the decision-making process. The limits come primarily from case law, which provides probationers, prison inmates, and parolees with due process when their freedom or potential freedom is put in jeopardy by sanctions from the system for alleged violations of the system's rules (*Morrissey v. Brewer, Mempa v. Rhay, Wolff v. McDonnell*). Theoretically, due process allows the offender to bring his information into the decision-making process while keeping unverified or biased information out. This keeps the decision-making mechanism less subject to the personal biases of probation and parole officers and prison personnel.

Morrissey v. Brewer, 408 U.S. 471 (1972), for example, allows parolees who are accused of violating the terms of their parole to have a quasi-judicial hearing in front of a hearing officer. That officer is usually an employee of the department of corrections. The parolees may be represented by an attorney or a friend, but they do not have the power of subpoena. However, they have the opportunity to challenge the information brought forward by their parole agents. *Wolff v. McDonnell,* 94 S. Ct. 2963 (1974), is organized similarly to *Morrissey* but applies before a prisoner can be punished for violating a prison rule. *Mempa v. Rhay,* 88 S. Ct. 254 (1967) applies to due process for probationeers. This tends to be more legal than Morrissey in that a court hearing is held and the probationeer is represented by an attorney who has the power of subpoena. The local prosecutor introduces the probation officer's evidence, and all witnesses testify under oath. To futher protect offenders being considered for sentencing, most states require that the defense attorney be given a copy of the presentence investigation prepared by the probation officer. The defense attorney thus can challenge any information or conclusions in the presentence investigation report that appear to be inaccurate or based on bias. For those who believe in limiting the discretion of criminal justice practitioners in probation, sentencing, and parole, all may appear to be well.

LIMITS OF LIMITING DISCRETION

Despite the rosy prognosis by some, however, it seems clear that attempts to control or eliminate discretion by case law, legislation, or even administrative decree will not survive the momentum of the criminal justice system. Legal and administrative changes will be resisted when they conflict with the role members of the criminal justice system have been socialized to accept. This is because practitioners within the system derive a sense of professionalism from their view of themselves as ones worthy of making decisions. Following a rigid set of imposed rules and guidelines will probably be viewed as a reduction in status from professional to paper pusher. The members of the criminal justice system will have normative commitments to the status quo and will avoid change — however "legal" the change is. Discretion will be clung to by ignoring the law when possible or by changing the focus of decision making within the system when the law cannot be ignored.

It may be difficult to accept the idea that those who comprise the criminal justice system and have obtained their authority from the law would attempt to circumvent it. One would assume that part of a criminal justice practitioner's socialization process would be to conform to legal limits. Looking at the criminal justice system in terms of administrative and organizational theory can further explain the resistance to change.

Criminal justice agencies usually are structured around a traditional bureaucratic hierarchy. A clear chain of command exists, with written policy and procedure spelling out the amount of authority delegated to organizational members. Duties are spelled out, and rules and regulations are relied on to control the performance of duties. The policies, procedures, descriptions of duties, and rules and regulations are developed at the top of the organization and imposed downward. The implicit assumption is that the work environment is stable and tasks can be carried out routinely.[6]

This type of structure presents no problem if the work environment is at least perceived as stable by the workers in direct contact with the environment, and if the organizational goals, policies, and procedures are viewed as valid by those performing the actual work. However, organizations will lose some degree of control over their workers if those workers perceive the situation to be one of nonroutine tasks in an unstable environment, or if they don't consider the organizational goals, policies, and the like as valid.[7] It is not unusual, for example, for a department of corrections to espouse a rehabilitation philosophy while the prison warden stresses control and parole officers, concerned with protection of society, stress a surveillance approach to parole supervision. The greater the divergence between the organization and its members' perceptions about what work should be done and how it should be done, the more likely it will be that the members will circumvent policy rules and regulations to perform what they think is the appropriate service. In short, if the organization and its members have different views of what social demands they are meeting, the members usually will ignore the formal organizational mandates and deliver the services they perceive as appropriate. The result is the creation within a bureaucracy of an informal organization with its own rules, leadership, communication system, and reward system.[8]

The development of a powerful informal organization is most likely to occur in large organizations in which the hierarchy consists of many layers between policymakers at the top and workers at the bottom levels. In this case filtering of communications through the hierarchy adds to the problems of control. Workers at the bottom level may get interpretations of policy and procedure that differ from their original intent. Accurate information about actual job performance may not reach top management levels, thereby making evaluations and control impossible. In large organizations where work is structurally dispersed, attempts at central administration are weakened as workers take on the norms of their immediate work environment, thus making control over organizational members by some uniform central decree unlikely.[9] Organizations may put more and more resources into methods of control; however, subordinates usually will put equally increasing and skilled efforts into circumventing control.[10]

Attempting to impose limits on discretion in the sentencing and parole processes is analogous to problems an organization has in getting its members to conform to policies and procedures. While it is not likely that those who wish to impose controls on discretion give thought to the stability of the criminal justice work environment, rigid controls can only have realistic applications to a work environment that is stable, or at least perceived as stable by criminal justice system members. If, for example, probation officers and judges feel sentencing must be done on a case-by-case basis, attempts to create broad offender categories and to sentence offenders within each category similarly will be fervently resisted.

Practitioners may feel that the imposed controls are not valid. The judges in Michigan's Upper Peninsula may be happy to have uniform sentencing through-out the state based on their standards, but the judges in Detroit would not accept those standards as reasonable. They would attempt to find ways to circumvent such standards and they probably would be successful.

As in a large bureaucracy, the imposition of controls at the top level — in this case from legislation and case law — may conveniently be reinterpreted as the new set of rules filters down to the practitioners. Conversely, information about covert methods of circumventing the new set of rules will not be readily passed upward, keeping the rule violator from scrutiny and control.

WAYS AND MEANS OF CIRCUMVENTING LIMITS

Having briefly discussed why criminal justice practitioners probably will ig-nore or modify attempts to impose limits on their decision-making powers, it is logical to describe some of the methods that can and are used to avoid control. If some form of flat sentencing for criminal offenders is substituted for the indeter-minant sentence, parole would be eliminated, as would be parole decision mak-ing. Presumably, discretion in sentencing would similarly be eliminated. However, the system has several ways of altering actual sentence length, thus keeping the prerogatives of judging offenders on a case-by-case basis. (*System* is defined as the natural interaction between police, prosecutor's office, probation department, and judges in a given jurisdiction.)

The police officer is considered the gatekeeper of the criminal justice system, because it is that individual who decides who will be arrested under what set of circumstances. Bittner describes the role of the police "as a mechanism for distri-bution of non-negotiable coercive force employed in accordance with the dictates of an intuitive grasp of situational exigencies."[11] One of the "situational exigen-cies" that weighs in an officer's decision to arrest or not is the likely response of the prosecutor's office and the courts to a particular type of arrest or surrounding circumstances. If the officer perceives that the rest of the system will treat the offender unjustly, he will weigh that perception in his decision. If from his point of view the offender will be treated too harshly, he may arrest for a lesser charge or not arrest at all. Or, if he feels that the system will treat the offender too leniently, he may choose to aggravate the arrest circumstances to create sufficient corollary charges, thereby increasing the likelihood of what he considers a just sentence.

One illustration of the process of police officers mitigating justice involves a small community in Ohio. There a new municipal court judge announced that all drivers convicted of drunk driving would receive the maximum fine and jail sentence regardless of circumstances or the offender's status. One year later the judge proudly announced that the arrest rates for drunk driving were down by some astounding figure. What really took place was that the law enforcement officers would not cite anyone for drunk driving unless they felt the offender deserved the punishment the court guaranteed. Conversely, most police officers can escalate a minor arrest into a major or multiple arrest if they so choose. By escalating a case the officer gives the prosecutor a strong plea-bargaining position. When the bargaining is settled, however, the probation department and the judge are given an offender who has the earmarks of a candidate for incarceration.

Through more than a century of practice, prosecuting attorneys have gained discretionary powers almost as broad as those police officers use in handling their case load. To facilitate plea bargaining they may overcharge, reduce or drop charges, and threaten to intervene or not to intervene in the sentencing process. Their reaction to flat sentencing may be to overcharge or reduce charges in the interest of seeing that offenders receive their "just" desserts, as well as to facilitate plea bargaining. In the case of presumptive sentencing, the prosecutors will play a crucial role in bringing information to the courts to determine mitigating or aggravating circumstances. While limiting judicial discretion in sentencing, both flat sentences and presumptive sentences provide prosecuting attorneys additional cards to play in plea bargaining. In effect, instead of being limited, discretion in sentencing has the potential for moving from the judiciary to the already powerful prosecutor's office.

The judges may be the least happy of all the players about having their decision making controlled. They can circumvent controls by playing within the rules or by ignoring them. They may reduce or change charges to allow them to give sentences that they feel are just or appropriate. In many states, rape and arson are nonprobational offenses. However, it is not uncommon to find rapists and arsonists walking the streets on probation after having their charges reduced by the sentencing judge to assault and battery and malicious destruction of property, both probational offenses. Judges may create harsher sentences by sentencing multiple charges consecutively. An extreme example of this occurred in a small town in southern Ohio when the town "troublemaker" pleaded guilty to thirteen misdemeanors. He was sentenced to 30 days on each count to run consecutively, a total of 390 days.

Due process has, for inmates, been imposed on the prison system (*Wolff v. McDonnell*) in an attempt to limit the discretion of guards. If a guard maintains an inmate has committed an offense, the inmate is called before a hearing officer. The hearing officer is not officially part of the custodial or treatment staff, a fact making him impartial, at least ideally. The inmate may attempt to refute the guard's evidence at the hearing. He may have other inmates testifying in his behalf and he may have a fellow inmate act as his advocate during the hearing. This does remove much of the guard's formal discretion. With this system guards undoubtedly lose some cases, and many guards may not report rule violations because of the perceived hassle of going through the hearing procedure. However, prison guards still are mandated to keep their cell blocks orderly and clean. To do so, rewards and punishments still are used, but at a different level.

First, there is little question that guards must depend on inmate leaders to keep order, in effect delegating part of their authority to the inmates. As guards perceive their authority eroding as their discretion becomes limited, an alternative that will be used is to delegate more of their authority to inmate leaders. It takes little imagination to understand how the troublemakers will be handled. The second possible approach is to use the prison counseling staff as a vehicle for rewards and punishment. While much is said about the treatment-versus-custody conflict in a prison, it is probably more philosophical than operational. Counselors are very much a part of the prison environment, and they will identify with some of the informal norms. It is therefore possible and probable that guards will seek and often gain the assistance of a counselor in dealing with a troublemaker. For example, guards can and do ask counselors to talk to particular problem inmates. The hope is that the inmate's behavior will manifest itself on a report in his file, written in psychological jargon, that will paint a negative picture of the inmate. Another approach is for a guard to gain the sympathy of an inmate who has rapport with the counselor (behavior modification usually works in this direction in a prison setting). That inmate may lead the counselor to believe that inmate Jones has a bad attitude, thus producing negative reports about Jones. If a prison system is not overcrowded, such reports will jeopardize an inmate's chances for parole.

The probation officer is an important and powerful component of the sentencing process. In states where flat sentencing prevails, the option of placing an offender on probation will continue to exist and probation officers (POs) will continue to be important. The key to the PO's power is in the presentence investigation (PSI). This document is the probation officer's summary of information about the defendant and recommendation as to sentencing. There is usually a high correlation between the PO's recommendation and the actual sentence. One study reports a correlation of 0.95 percent.[12] Several explanations for this high correlation exist, but it is sufficient to state here that the PSI is an important document in sentencing.

Traditionally, the PSI was held as confidential information between the probation department and the court. Neither the defendant nor the defense attorney was privy to the documents. The defendant, at the mercy of the probation officer, could only hope he would write an impartial, objective PSI. Even with a fair PO there was no way of knowing whether the information he received was accurate or honest. Thus the system moved to disclosure of the PSI to the defense attorney and the defendant, allowing the information in the PSI to be challenged. In addition, the PO could no longer promise confidentiality to information sources.

This often creates a dilemma for the PO. He may have access to information that seems significant in a sentencing decision but that may create a threat to the information source. This dilemma is usually resolved by passing the information on to the sentencing judge verbally, a procedure that is strictly illegal. From a practical standpoint, one might ask why probation officers and judges would put themselves in jeopardy by intentionally violating the defendant's rights. The answer is simple. The process is nearly impossible to detect and it brings information to the court that otherwise would not be revealed.

One might consider the ethics or morality involved in members of the court intentionally violating a defendant's rights. When the rights of an offender are weighed against what appears to be the very likely harm to society, the morality is easily rationalized: the letter of the law should not subvert the purpose of the system.

A significant part of a probation and parole officer's duties in supervising offenders is surveillance of their behavior. If the offenders violate the terms of their supervision, the PO may take action such as counseling or arrest, or revoking the offender's probation. Except in very visible cases, POs have almost total discretion in who not to arrest and/or facilitate revocation. Historically, revoking an offender's probation or parole was almost totally in the hands of the probation or parole offices. However, case law has effectively limited that extreme discretion by providing probationeers and parolees who face revocation proceedings with a form of due process (*Mempa v. Rhay; Morrissey v. Brewer*).

With due process, probation revocation hearings are held before a judge, with all testimony given under oath. The probationeer is entitled to an attorney; in the case of an indigent probationeer, the court will appoint one. Parole revocation hearings are not as formal. Evidence is presented to a hearing officer who is an employee of that parole system. Testimony is not given under oath and, while parolees may be represented by an attorney, most states will not pay for one. (One exception is the state of Michigan—*Hawken v. Michigan*.) However, for the PO who wishes to be arbitrary, due process is more of a nuisance than an impediment. It is nearly impossible for the typical offender to consistently conform to all the conditions of probation and parole. With rigorous surveillance by the PO and police agencies, and good bookkeeping by the PO, a revocation case eventually can be built against most offenders. This process does take place, especially when an offender is perceived in a negative light by the PO.

REDEFINING DISCRETION: PARTICIPATION AND COMMITMENT

Although a bleak picture has been painted, offenders today probably are treated more equitably than they were in the past. I began working in corrections as a parole officer in southern Ohio in 1964. At that time I heard war stories about the good old days when a few more law-and-order-oriented POs would return parolees to prison for the slightest rule infraction. It was not uncommon for parolees to be taken out of their homes or off their jobs, belly chained and handcuffed, and driven directly back to prison. At a later, convenient date, the PO would write a report for the parole board setting forth the reasons why the parolee was returned.

This type of arbitrary case-load management does not exist today. At least a parolee must be provided with the trappings of due process. In fact, most contemporary POs probably would be totally opposed to subjecting parolees to such arbitrary and total power. Therein lies an important consideration: normative commitment is the major form of control in an organization where members perceive themselves as professionals.[13] If arbitrary and disparate application of discretion in the criminal justice system is to be minimized, the decision makers in the system must have some normative commitments to the methods developed for that purpose. Without some commitment to dealing with disparate decision making, most methods developed are likely to prove ineffective.

To gain the commitment of criminal justice practitioners to a system limiting their discretion, the best approach is to put the problem in their hands. This step may be a costly one, but it is necessary. If a system of controlling discretion is to a great extent developed by those it is intended to control, acceptance is far more likely than if the system is imposed externally by the courts or by legislation.

The drawback with this approach is that it suggests a proactive, rather than reactive, posture on the part of the criminal justice system, its components, and its members. The system, however, by virtue of its duties and its subservient posture to politics, is more reactive to dealing with problems. Although more and more administrators in the system are getting formal management training oriented toward proactive problem solving, the realization that most pressure for change is external is cause for pessimism about the criminal justice system and its members' willingness to participate in policy decisions affecting the system's destiny.

If this analysis is correct, external attempts to control the application of discretion by criminal justice practitioners will be successfully resisted. It is incumbent upon those who are leaders in changing and creating discretionary policy to actively seek participation on the part of criminal justice practitioners. In Michigan, for example, a sentencing guidelines study recently has been completed. Essentially, judges' sentencing patterns in regard to felony charges were examined to determine what sentencing disparities exist under what conditions. The next step will be to bring representatives of the Michigan judiciary together to discuss findings and development of sentencing guidelines. Whether the guidelines are mandated by legislation or imposed by judicial norms and peer pressures, the active participation of the judiciary will vastly increase the likelihood that the guidelines will be followed.

In conclusion, using a strictly legalistic or administrative approach to impose limits on discretion will not be effective unless an agency is created to search out and punish practitioners who violate the legal limits of discretion. The development of such an agency with the power and resources it needs to function effectively is unlikely. For successful implementation of policy changes that limit discretion in the criminal justice system, those being controlled will have to participate in policy making.

CHAPTER EIGHT

Judicial Oversight of Discretion in the Prison System

JON M. KINNAMON

THE ADMINISTRATION of penal institutions is an aspect of the criminal justice system where, perhaps more than any other area, discretion has been unreviewed and unfettered, at least until recent years. The traditional policy of the courts with respect to complaints of inmates has been described as "hands off." This attitude gradually evolved from the notion that incarceration strips inmates of their constitutional rights and birthrights; that is, a prisoner has the status of "a slave of the state" with no rights.[1]

As a result of this hands-off approach, prisoners for many years were subject to the institutional administration's unbridled discretion, with review and intervention by the courts only in the most extreme circumstances of abuse. As late as 1950 one federal court declared a policy of review of a state prison administration's discretion only upon a showing of the most egregious conduct by prison officials: "This Court is prepared to protect State prisoners *from death or serious bodily harm* in the hands of prison authorities, but is not prepared to establish itself as a 'co-administrator' of state prisons along with the duly appointed State officials." (emphasis added)[2]

The initial "slave of the state" notion gradually has been transformed into a concept that "a prisoner retains all the rights of an ordinary citizen except those expressly, or by necessary implication, taken from him by law."[3] According to the "retention" theory, an inmate is not entitled to all the privileges and protections against arbitrariness enjoyed by free men. The concept proceeds upon a recognition that "lawful incarceration brings about necessary withdrawal or limitation of many privileges and rights, a retraction justified by the considerations underlying our penal system."[4]

Most recently, constitutionally grounded attacks by inmates on prison officials' discretionary powers appear to have been effective in achieving judicial review. One of the most important cases providing a delineation of inmates'

Jon M. Kinnamon, attorney, Cedar Rapids and Iowa City, Iowa.

constitutional status, and delineation of the constitutional limits on penal administrators' discretion, is *Wolff v. McDonnell*. *Wolff* involved allegations that
Nebraska Penal and Correctional Complex disciplinary procedures did not comply
with the Due Process Clause of the Fourteenth Amendment. *Wolff* brought
directly into issue areas of prison administration that previously had not been
considered by the federal judiciary. *Wolff* is significant because of its discussion of
the inmates' constitutional status:

> Lawful imprisonment necessarily makes unavailable many rights and
> privileges of the ordinary citizen, a "retraction justified by the considerations
> underlying our penal system." *Price v. Johnston,* 334 U.S. 266, 285 (1948).
> But though his rights may be diminished by the needs and exigencies of the
> institutional environment, a prisoner is not wholly stripped of constitutional
> protections when he is imprisoned for crime. There is no iron curtain drawn
> between the Constitution and the prisons of this country. Prisoners have been
> held to enjoy substantial religious freedom under the First and Fourteenth
> Amendments.... They retain right of access to the courts.... Prisoners are
> protected under the Equal Protection Clause of the Fourteenth Amendment
> from invidious discrimination based on race.... Prisoners may also claim the
> protections of the Due Process Clause. They may not be deprived of life,
> liberty, or property without due process of law....
>
> Of course, as we have indicated, the fact that prisoners retain rights
> under the Due Process Clause in no way implies that these rights are not
> subject to restrictions imposed by the nature of the regime to which they have
> been lawfully committed....
>
> In sum, there must be mutual accommodation between institutional
> needs and objectives and the provisions of the constitution that are of general
> application.[5]

The *Wolff* case provides legal recognition of the rights and privileges possessed by a prison inmate and safeguards the essential democratic right of a citizen
inside or outside prison walls: human dignity. *Wolff* recognizes that security and
institutional needs may require special restrictions on an inmate. However, such
restrictions must be justified in the first instance, and the justification for the
restrictions must continue during the entirety of their imposition. An aspect of the
Wolff case almost as important as the recognition of the scope of the inmate's
constitutional rights is the Supreme Court's declaration that the judiciary is a
proper forum for enforcement of constitutional guarantees against infringements
by state penal system officials. Although courts will intervene only when the
consequence of a discretionary act attains constitutional dimensions, judiciary
intervention provides the best remedy to assure that prison officials establish and
abide by fair and objective administrative rules, and that the rules themselves, as
well as any discretionary acts, are constitutionally sound.

In Iowa, two recent prison cases exemplify the role of the judiciary in providing discretionary oversight: *Kelly v. Brewer* and *Clark v. Brewer.*[6] These decisions
illustrate the evolution of the role of the judicial branch in overseeing the operation of the Iowa State Penitentiary (ISP) and, specifically, in regard to Administrative Solid Lockup (ASL).

Administrative Solid Lockup involves the exercise of administrative judgment in determining whether an individual inmate should be segregated from the general prison population. Also involved is the prediction of what he will do or what will be done to him if he remains in the general population or is returned to it after a period of segregation. Unlike punitive segregation imposed by a prison administration as punishment for an inmate's misconduct, administrative segregation is not a punitive measure. Necessary for a number of nonpunitive reasons, ASL holds individual inmates in segregated status for varying, indefinite periods of time. As practiced by the ISP, it is a form of solitary confinement, and as the Eighth Circuit Court of Appeals observed in *Kelly v. Brewer:*

> [A]dministrative segregation is not inherently unconstitutional, its validity depends upon the relative humaneness of the conditions of the segregated confinement and in individual cases upon the existence of a valid and subsisting reason or reasons for the segregation, such as protection of the segregated inmates from other inmates, protection of other inmates and prison personnel from the segregated inmates, prevention of escapes and similar reasons.

It is incumbent upon the prison administration to show that the denial of the inmate's liberty is rationally related to the state's interest in maintaining the security of the institution. At the heart of the *Kelly* decision at both tiers of the federal judiciary was the awareness of two defects in the existing ISP-ASL system: no meaningful review of an inmate's ASL classification, and the prison administration's possession of an unbridled discretion to retain a disliked inmate continuously in indefinite ASL status.

In separating an inmate from the general population of the penal institution, administrative segregation almost always imposes upon the segregated inmate severe restraints. The placement of an inmate in ASL is psychologically intimidating and physically taxing on the prisoner's well-being. Unavailability and inaccessibility to essential goods, services, and privileges enjoyed by the general prison population constitute such fundamental deprivations that their denial must be done in a manner consistent with the federal constitution.

The list of interests that may be affected by administrative segregation is awesome: availability of sinks, toilets, beds, and bedding; availability, number, and nature of meals served in ASL compared to those for the general population, as well as availability of seconds and desserts, and preparation and service of food at proper temperatures; allowance of canteen privileges; allowance of clothing compared to that for the general population, and frequency of change; allowance and frequency of showers; availability and frequency of exercise and recreational privileges; availability of library privileges, movie privileges, mail privileges (sending and receiving), visitation privileges (other inmates or outsiders), and telephone privileges; allowance of employment opportunities inside the institution (character of employment, duration, and wages); availability of educational opportunities or technical and vocational training; allowance of religious services and activities; availability of cultural, social, or self-help activities; availability of personal and group counseling; availability of hobby and craft opportunities; allowance of personal possessions to be retained in ASL (television, radio, books, and materials); availability of medical care and medical checkups upon request; availability of inmate protection from tear gassing by regulation or supervisory oversight and approval; availability of the right to privacy and protection of the segregated inmate from indiscriminate searches and/or indiscriminate observation; allowance of freedom from physical restraint, such as handcuffs or shackles; and lastly, availability of periodic reviews of the ASL classification as well as dissemination to the segregated inmate upon the conclusion of each review of the reason for ASL termination or continuation.

Besides the issue of whether administrative segregation is justified in each case, the curtailment or elimination of any of these rights and privileges seriously alters the segregated inmate's conditions as compared to those of the general prison population. Deprivation of these interests necessitates that the manner of their denial be fair and lawful.

The leading case on the topic of administrative segregation and due process violation in the discretionary implementation of ASL procedures is *Kelly v. Brewer.* Here some background is in order. On June 8, 1972, Warner Kelly, an inmate at ISP, stabbed and killed a prison guard. After that incident Kelly was confined in "indefinite administrative segregation," an equivalent of ASL, on the ground that he was dangerous to the security and good order of the penitentiary. In 1973 Kelly filed a lawsuit in the U.S. District Court for the Southern District of Iowa, alleging, inter alia, that "there is no meaningful review of [my] status in 'administrative segregation' and that there are no meaningful standards to determine when [I] should be released from 'administrative segregation.' " He contended that these grievances constituted a violation of due process.

The district court agreed with Kelly and ordered the defendant, Lou V. Brewer, then warden of ISP, to develop and promulgate meaningful standards for reviewing Kelly's status. The district court's concern centered on the warden's existing administrative segregation system—namely, the "indefinite administrative segregation" status. On appeal, the Eighth Circuit Court held that Warden Brewer would be permitted to place and retain Kelly in lockup if the warden first conducted an "appropriate evaluation" and reported his determination to the district court, setting out his reasons and identifying the criteria and standards employed in reaching his determination.

Also important is the case of *Clark v. Brewer,* which followed the Kelly ruling. At the time of the initiation of his lawsuit, plaintiff Edward Clark had been confined in the ISP at Fort Madison since February 1960. He was twenty-two years old when he was initially incarcerated for armed robbery. Upon initiation of his lawsuit in 1979, he was forty-one. During the first ten to twelve years of confinement, Clark did not behave acceptably within the ISP or at the Iowa Security Medical Facility. He received numerous disciplinary reports for infractions of institutional rules; much more serious, he stabbed and killed another ISP inmate in 1965 and was convicted of second-degree murder. He also stabbed and killed a guard in April 1969 and was later convicted of first-degree murder. Subsequent to the 1969 stabbing, Clark was placed in ASL within ISP, where he remained through the filing and determination of his lawsuit, over ten years later.

Prior to the *Kelly* decision of the federal judiciary, the ISP prison administration had unbridled discretion in determining the placement of an inmate in ASL. This procedure allowed an inmate to be placed in ASL for any reason, including punishment or the satisfaction of personal vindictiveness. Likewise, a segregated inmate could be subjected to inhumane conditions, without recourse to any meaningful or immediate remedy or impartial review. Unfettered discretion in the hands of prison officials had the consequence of depriving an inmate of knowledge both of the reasons for an ASL classification and of the basis for comparing his treatment with others placed in ASL before him; these circumstances prevented any application of objective standards whereby an inmate could reasonably antici- pate release from ASL through certain behavior. An inmate in ASL never knew what objective criteria would be used by prison officials to evaluate his ability to conform to the rules and regulations of the institution—criteria that would be necessary to fairly determine the inmate's release to the general population or to extend his freedom and entitlements.

In their review of prison administration procedures, courts demonstrate an acute awareness of the difficulties facing prison authorities and the pragmatic reasons advanced for keeping in ASL prisoners who have killed others within the prison walls. However, the courts have ruled that such concerns do not satisfy the federal constitution. Use of ASL may not be based on notions of punishment, deterrence, or fear of adverse staff reaction. Instead, it must be for the articulated purpose of maintaining the security of the institution. The Eighth Circuit Court has ruled that due process considerations limit "unbridled discretion" exercised by prison officials.

In *Kelly,* the Eighth Circuit Court held that an inmate may be a threat to the security at one time but not at another time: "It should be emphasized that the reason or reasons for segregation must not only be valid at the outset but must continue to subsist during the period of segregation."

The federal judiciary balks at becoming a coadministrator of state prisons. Intervention of the courts is invoked only when constitutional questions are at issue. Before the *Kelly* decision, there existed no review of the prison administra- tion's ASL classification and no protection of the inmate's constitutional guaran- tees. Judicial oversight became the sole mechanism for revamping ASL policy.

The *Kelly* decision, based on due process grounds, required the prison ad- ministration to adopt a single plan setting forth the factors to be considered periodically by prison officials in determining if a prisoner's ASL status should be continued. The Eighth Circuit Court ruled that such a plan could not be so subjective in nature that it allowed arbitrary decision making in violation of the inmate's right to substantive due process. As a result, the warden or the prison administration retained discretion in determining if an inmate's ASL status should continue, but the exercise of the discretion had to be within an objective frame- work.

Periodic review necessitates procedural safeguards. Written notice to an in- mate of the time of a review hearing and the nature of the review is a minimal requirement. An inmate's opportunity to present evidence and to call witnesses if the prison officials so agree or state regulations or procedures so authorize are critical to a fair review.

A federal district court has held that prison officials must provide an inmate with a gradually increased degree of freedom under controlled circumstances. In this way a reasoned decision can be made based on empirical evidence that an inmate in administrative segregation is fit for release. This procedure was viewed in the case of *Mims v. Shapps*, 457 F Supp. 247 (WD Pa. 1978), as a minimal requirement in order to accord an inmate substantive due process. The thrust of *Mims* is to compel prison officials to provide a program for objectively evaluating an inmate's progress. Without this procedure, the initial rationale for imposition of ASL could become, by acquiescence, the sole rationale for its continuation, and any change in the inmate's conduct would go unnoticed and unevaluated. In such a situation illusory reasons for ASL retention often become substitutes for real ones.

Although the acts for which the inmate was initially confined in ASL may be properly considered "as historical facts of [his] case and as factors to be considered, among others, in determining whether after a lapse of months or even years it is safe to terminate [his] segregated status," these acts may not be given "artificial weight" or become "determining or preponderant guidelines" in deciding whether or not the inmate can safely be returned to the general population.

In *Kelly,* the Eighth Circuit Court expressly disregarded Warden Brewer's assertion that an inmate convicted of killing a member of the prison staff thereby became a "fit subject for administrative segregation for a prolonged and indefinite period of time and perhaps for the duration of his term of imprisonment." This view was faulty precisely because it failed to recognize that conduct can change during imprisonment, just as it can change anywhere. Because valid reasons for continued confinement in ASL must be based on current information about the inmate, prison officials are compelled to have contact with the inmate. Specifically, valid reasons to extend an inmate's ASL status must be based on articulable, informed judgment. An obligation thus is imposed on the authorities to increase the amount of information available on the inmate's present attitude and behavior.

Reasons for continuation of ASL are required, in part, to facilitate later review both administrative and judicial. This approach provides the affected inmate with a rationale for the prison administration's decision, and prevents arbitrary discretionary acts by requiring an evidentiary basis for the decision. Meaningful review of an inmate's ASL status requires an impartial decision maker. At a minimum, the decision maker should not have made up his mind in advance as to what the outcome will be.[7] The inmate should be assured that the judgment and review involved in the decision-making process is objectively verified. The burden is on the prison authorities to show that a reasonable and reliable determination was made that a particular inmate presented a significantly greater risk to prison security than do the inmates within the general prison population. In *Clark,* the court found that the inmate's constitutional rights were violated as a result of Warden Brewer's failure to review monthly the inmate's segregation and to provide him with recommendations as to how he might change his status. The prison administration's own plan required that the defendants do so, yet the prison administrators had failed to abide by it.

According to Section 4382, *Manual of Standards for Adult Correctional Institutions,* Commission on Accreditation for Corrections, 1977:

> Written policy and procedure provide that inmates in administrative segregation are reviewed by the classification committee or other authorized staff groups every seven days for the first two months and at least every 30 days thereafter... The hearing should determine whether the reasons for initial placement in the unit still exist. If they do not, the inmate should be released from the unit. Provisions should be made for the inmate to appear at the hearing.

In both the *Kelly* and *Clark* cases, the inmates were concerned about ASL review hearings becoming a sham or being subverted from their intended purpose. Rather than a review of the ASL classification, their complaints contended that the focus of review hearing had shifted to a "welfare review" during which the inmate could lodge any complaints about his surroundings or relate any adverse experiences with prison personnel. The main criticism levied by *Clark* was that many of the review procedures established by the prison in response to the court order in *Kelly* were completely ignored in his case. With the *Kelly* ruling, prison officials were obligated to recommend to Clark what factors would be used to evaluate him in future determinations of his ASL classification and his standing as a security risk. The findings and recommendations of the prison administration were to be given to him in writing, but in fact they were not. Plaintiff Clark contended in his lawsuit that ten years passed without either a semiannual review, an annual review, or an annual psychiatric reevaluation.

In an order in the *Clark* case, dated April 21, 1980, the Southern District of Iowa determined that the defendants' current plan for review of inmates in ASL for possible release to ISP's general population (GP) violated plaintiff's substantive and procedural due process rights. Relying on the Eighth Circuit's *Kelly* opinion, the court concluded that the criteria applied by defendants were so subjective in nature that the decision whether to continue an inmate in ASL would not be rationally related to the stated goals of ASL placement. (ASL is the progenitor for Close Management [CM].) The court directed the defendants to prepare and submit guidelines for determining in a rational manner whether an inmate should be retained in ASL.

The court also ruled that defendants' indefinite continuation of plaintiff in ASL violated his procedural due process rights. In its findings the court determined that the plaintiff had been given no opportunity to show his ability to conform to GP living and no guidance on how he could attempt to prove his rehabilitation in ASL. The court ordered the defendants to prepare a plan setting forth the minimal procedural protections that would be afforded ASL inmates in the review decision-making process, including provisions for periodic review, for explaining proper modes of showing rehabilitation, for ASL inmates' right to compel witnesses to testify at review hearings, and for allowing conforming inmates an opportunity to prove their increasing ability to conform to the standards of life in GP.

Subsequently the relief awarded Clark was bifurcated and instituted at different stages. On July 13, 1981, the parties filed a stipulation indicating Edward Clark had received $7,000.00 in satisfaction of Clark's claim for monetary damages. As part of the same stipulation, Clark stated he would enter a request for voluntary dismissal with prejudice upon the court's final acceptance of a plan for the review of inmates in CM.

The parties held discussions as to the minimal requirements for the ASL review plan and were close to agreement, when on February 22, 1983, the U.S. Supreme Court decided *Hewitt v. Helms.*[8] Though several procedures had already been accepted by the defendants and integrated in defendants' CM, the district court was requested to rule on the issues still in dispute and to resolve any conflict between the legal conclusions reached in *Hewitt* and those reached in *Kelly* and to apply the requested analysis to the facts of the *Clark* case.

The district court's final order in *Clark,* dated December 19, 1983, reflected a careful review of the legal and factual findings employed in *Kelly* and *Hewitt.* *Kelly* indicated that in a prison setting an inmate acquired a protected liberty interest in remaining in the GP, an interest independently protected by due process. Though this constitutional premise was rejected by the U.S. Supreme Court in *Hewitt,* the analysis of *Kelly,* declaring illegal the arbitrary continuation of an inmate's solitary confinement, is still valid under the due process test established in *Hewitt.*

In *Hewitt,* the U.S. Supreme Court required a court to examine applicable state statutes, regulations, and procedures for confining an inmate to administrative segregation and to determine if the laws, regulations, and procedures recognized a liberty interest that should be accorded due process protections. In light of the mandatory nature of the state statutes, regulations, and procedures under review in *Hewitt* setting forth the policy for confining an inmate to administrative segregation, the U.S. Supreme Court ruled that an inmate within this particular prison system had acquired a protected liberty interest in remaining in the general prison population and that due process protections attached. Whether state laws, regulations, or the practices of prison officials provide prisoners a justifiable expectation that they will remain in the general prison population is a critical factor in evaluating the existence of a protected liberty interest. However, any judicial review must use caution in raising privileges and freedoms granted as part of administration policy to constitutional levels by the virtue of that policy itself.

The legal philosophy in *Hewitt* defers to prison administrators. The U.S. Supreme Court held that prison officials should be accorded wide-ranging deference in adoption and execution of policies and practices that in their judgment are needed to preserve internal order and discipline and to maintain institutional security. The legal philosophy inherent in the minority holding in *Hewitt,* and implicit in the Court's decision in *Kelly,* is that the touchstone of due process is the protection of the individual against arbitrary action of government. Such a philosophy originates from an evaluation of the conditions and restrictions in administrative confinement and a comparison of these conditions and restrictions with those that are experienced by inmates in the GP. As a basis for this view, administrative confinement singles out an inmate for more severe restraints not specified in the original criminal sentence; an inmate placed in a security cell for administrative reasons suffers a severe impairment of the residium of liberty that he enjoyed as a prisoner in the GP—impairment that triggers the requirement for due process safeguards.

Within the judicial environment of the *Hewitt* and *Kelly* decisions, the district court on December 19, 1983, entered its final order in the *Clark* case. The court reaffirmed the procedural protections afforded an inmate in *Kelly*, but did so upon the due process grounds established in *Hewitt*. The district court noted that the express purpose for defendants' implementation of the current CM policy is

> Controlling of the intractable inmate, who by his behavior has identified himself as assaultive, predacious, riotous or disruptive to the institution...[and] [t]o impress upon these inmates th[at] inappropriate behavior will not be acceptable at the Iowa State Penitentiary and that only through acceptable behavior can they earn their gradual release and return to the general population of the Penitentiary.

Because prison officials had limited their discretion by requiring that this or a similar substantive predicate exist before an inmate is retained in CM, this self-imposed discretionary restriction lends support to the expectation of a liberty interest on the part of the prisoners.

The district court declared that the overriding issue in *Clark* was whether an ISP inmate, once placed in CM, possessed a liberty interest in not being retained indefinitely in CM that was protected by the due process clause. In absence of federal statute, the due process clause had to provide the basis for procedural safeguards to limit indefinite confinement or the court was without power to act.

The *Clark* decision recognized that new Iowa law, long-established prison policy, and recently adopted prison regulations created a liberty interest in not being indefinitely retained in CM. Since defendants' management control system limited educational and employment opportunities of inmates who spend time in CM, the inmates' efforts to realize their statutory right to five-days-per-month good conduct time would be hindered by retention in CM. In addition to the new legislation, affecting those inmates convicted after July 1, 1983, the *Clark* court ruled that a liberty interest was involved with inmates convicted prior to July 1, 1983. The court ruled that long-standing prison policy and current written regulations vest all other inmates with a protected liberty interest; ISP officials had followed an unwritten policy since at least 1974 that there must be an express reason for retaining an inmate in CM. Concluding that ISP inmates possessed a liberty interest protected by the due process clause, the court determined what procedures the defendants must afford the inmates in order to provide constitutional protection to that interest. The court considered the private and governmental interests at stake in the CM review process and the value of specific procedural requirements for that process.

The *Clark* decision emphasized that the defendants in the CM review decision-making process would not be faced with exigent circumstances. There existed a distinction between being placed in CM and being retained in CM. After the inmate was placed in CM where he ceased to be a security threat, the need for immediate action to preserve security was eliminated. In *Hewitt,* the issue of indefinite administrative segregation was not addressed. Although the *Hewitt* Court concluded that the inmate's fifty-day term in administrative segregation did not infringe his liberty interest, the *Clark* court ruling addressed the possibility of inmates seeking review of CM confinement after months or years of confinement in CM. The length of incarceration in CM is an element that affects the weight of the inmate's liberty interest. Inmates' interest in being granted greater privileges or in being released to GP increases the longer they are retained in CM. Continuous confinement in CM adversely affects the ISP inmate's ability to earn good conduct time, lengthening his term of confinement at ISP itself. The heightened interest of prison officials recognized by the *Hewitt* Court in the context of initial placement in administrative segregation decreased substantially after the inmate had been placed in CM and was seeking a return to GP.

Following *Kelly,* the district court concluded review hearings are essential; without some method to check the progress of CM inmates, there is no ensuring that valid reasons continue to subsist during the period of segregation. However, the court found that although the value of frequent review hearings increases steadily for a time, it later decreases when the record of the inmate's conduct while in CM establishes that he is relatively incorrigible.

Inside the prison walls, ASL or CM constitutes the most isolated locality in our society. Government power may be used to restrict liberty to a maximum degree, and a liberty interest—a prerequisite for judicial review and entitlement to procedural safeguards—may be unrecognized in state law, regulations, rules, or practices of state officials.[9] If a liberty interest is recognized, such an interest may only provide a basis for very limited protection from indefinite confinement. Without access to the procedural protections of the federal constitution, an inmate's constitutional safeguards dissipate and governmental and penal interest become the sole concern. To render the federal constitution inapplicable to a category of citizens, based upon a finding that no state law, regulation, or practice recognizes a liberty interest in the placement and confinement of an inmate in CM, opens the door for state governments and prison administrators to revert to the "slave of the state" doctrine of unfettered discretion without review. Because many present state statutes, regulations, or practices may be interpreted as providing a liberty interest, and many laws, regulations, and prison practices affect prisoners in the general population as well as those confined in administrative segregation, reversion to a "slave of the state" status may prove a difficult course. As courts construe a liberty interest in applicable regulations and prison practices, these decisions solidify by judicial enforcement the interpreted liberty interest. In the event no liberty interest is found to exist by the courts, and legislatures and prison authorities adopt no measures in which a liberty interest is included, or follow practices from which one may be implied, then discretion in prison becomes easy to assess and prison officials will be held to a procedural "standard" of acting in any manner they want unless the procedure affects substantive due process rights.

CHAPTER NINE

Congressional Activity and Discretion in the Criminal Justice System

---

EDWARD I. SIDLOW and BETH M. HENSCHEN

DISCRETION underlies most of the key decisions made in the law implementation system. It is a pervasive part of a process that is charged with seeing that "justice is done." At all stages of the law implementation process, decision making is characterized by discretion rather than formality or certainty.[1] Much discussion has been directed toward the wide latitude that legal actors have in determining the fate of defendants and over the resultant disparity in treatment. Critics of the present system would favor procedural and administrative reforms that would severely restrict the number and extent of discretionary decisions made in the processing of criminal cases. Opponents of such reforms, on the other hand, argue that proposals to routinize the criminal justice process ignore the positive consequences of discretion, namely, flexibility and individualization of justice. For the most part, however, the debate over discretion has centered over the best way to replace discretionary decisions that are arbitrary and discriminatory with those that are not only inevitable but desirable.

Suggestions for reform have been directed at the exercise of discretion at all stages of the criminal justice process. Viewing police discretion as particularly critical because police are the initiating agency in a vast majority of cases, some reforms have focused on structuring police decisions to invoke the criminal process. As James LeGrande notes:

> Only rarely have police officers been provided with meaningful policies, instructions, or training in the utilization of their discretion. The legislatures have generally phrased their grants or limitations of power in broad terms; the police administrators have taken a course of permitting officers to improvise on

---

Edward I. Sidlow, Miami University, Oxford, Ohio.
Beth M. Henschen, Purdue University, West Lafayette, Indiana.

a case-by-case basis, and the courts' primary concern has been officers who exceed their arrest power.[2]

The President's Task Force on Police in the mid-1960s found the failure of police executives to formulate policy regarding the exercise of discretion to be a significant problem. As a remedy, it proposed that police departments develop clearly stated guidelines to aid rank-and-file patrol officers in making decisions in situations that require some exercise of discretion.[3] Very few departments, however, have implemented the task force proposals. For the most part, police continue to rely on personal judgments in encounters with suspects and complainants.

The development of internal policy guidelines also has been suggested as a means by which to limit prosecutorial discretion. While recognizing the need for flexibility and sensitivity in prosecutorial decision making, reformers also prize certainty, consistency, and an absence of the arbitrary exercise of discretionary power at critical stages of the criminal justice process. To achieve the desired balance between these two competing values, it has been proposed that offices of prosecution develop comprehensive and detailed policy statements to govern the exercise of prosecutorial decision making. While such formulated policy would not ensure absolute uniformity, some argue that it should facilitate the achievement of "tolerable consistency."[4]

Reform efforts also have been directed toward restraining the prosecutor's discretion in handling criminal defendants through plea bargaining, a power the prosecutor exercises in an exchange relationship with others in the courtroom work group. Perhaps the most controversial of the 1973 reforms suggested by the National Advisory Commission on Criminal Justice Standards and Goals was the complete abolition of plea negotiations.[5] While the commission's extreme position is a minority one, it nevertheless underscores the concern that many have in the face of the considerable discretionary power prosecutors possess in determining the fate of criminal defendants.

Limiting the discretion exercised by judges in setting bail, conducting the trial, and sentencing defendants also has been the focus of a significant number of reform proposals. Of greatest concern is the disparity in sentences imposed for similar offenses. Judicial discretion and sentencing disparity result from legislative policies that stipulate maximum and minimum thresholds, from indeterminate sentences, and from judges' own perceptions of the purpose and utility of legal policies.

A variety of proposals to control the abuses of discretionary sentencing power have been suggested. They include reducing the severity of the sentence in order to increase the certainty and immediacy of punishment, increasing the use of sentencing councils, and introducing appellate review of trial judge sentencing.[6] Major structural reforms also have been proposed. Most prominent are those that would eliminate indeterminate sentences and rely instead on either "flat-time sentencing," mandatory minimum sentences, or presumptive sentencing.[7]

Additional reform proposals are primarily procedural in nature; they call for a system in which the sentencing judge must consider certain goals and criteria articulated by Congress and must apply guidelines set forth by a commission on sentencing and corrections.[8] Some also seek to abolish sentence-modifying devices such as parole and "good time," because in most cases they duplicate the initial sentencing function, and they often lead to an abuse of discretionary power at a critical point in the criminal justice system. Parole boards often make no attempt to structure their decision making through rules, policy statements, or guidelines; the resultant variation and uncertainty in parole board decisions deprive a prisoner of the incentive to prepare seriously for release.

The number and variety of reforms aimed at structuring the exercise of discretion at key stages of the criminal justice process seem to suggest that many observers of the justice system view discretionary decision making as not just a part of the problem, but rather as the problem itself.[9] Suggestions for change, however, do not necessarily translate into actual reform of the system. Participants in the criminal justice process are not likely to institute reforms limiting their decision-making power. Moreover, because legislatures are intimately tied to the criminal justice system, adoption of many of the proposed changes would require legislative action. Legislative bodies create the structure of courts, define their jurisdiction, and provide resources for the operation of the criminal justice process. While all of these legislative functions help to determine how cases are handled, it is more important to note that legislatures also define criminal activity and provide the range of sentencing alternatives. Thus, limiting the exercise of discretion is in large measure a legislative task.

CONGRESSIONAL ATTEMPTS AT LIMITING DISCRETION

This section examines the activities that have taken place in Congress in order to limit judicial discretion. Data are drawn from the public record and covers a twenty-year period, 1960–1980.[10] The data include any attempt by Congress to restrict judicial discretion, and in this case *attempt* is broadly defined. In examining the whole of congressional activity, committee hearings, reports, and floor activities are considered, as well as legislation that became public law.

Relative to congressional activity in the past decade, the 1960s witnessed very few legislative attempts to limit judicial discretion. Rather, national attention was focused on the increasing incidence of street crime and legislative efforts were directed toward crime control. During this period, then, the emphasis was on expanding federal assistance to local law enforcement and criminal justice agencies to stem the rising crime rate. Congressional activity in this area culminated in the passage of the Omnibus Crime Control and Safe Streets Act of 1968, the most extensive anticrime legislation in the nation's history.

Congressional preoccupation with curbing crime was not matched by a comparable desire to limit the exercise of judicial discretion during the 1960s. There was, however, some acknowledgment of the discretionary "problem." In 1965, for example, the Senate passed and sent to the House a comprehensive measure authorizing new procedures for the release of federal prisoners charged with noncapital offenses. Signed into law one year later, the Bail Reform Act was the result of a growing concern among members of the judiciary and other criminal justice observers with the operation of federal bail procedures. Studies of bail systems had revealed that regardless of the likelihood of appearing for trial, prisoners who could afford bail were allowed to go free pending trial, while those who could not awaited trial in jail. The central feature of the Bail Reform Act was to require release, on either personal recognizance or unsecured bond, of persons charged with noncapital federal offenses unless the judicial officer concluded that there was not a reasonable assurance of appearance for trial. The act required the judicial officer to take into account a series of factors concerning both the nature of the crime and the criminal, thereby structuring the range of discretion that might be exercised by the officer in setting conditions for release.

Congressional concern with discretion during this first period also was expressed in legislation designed to permit the appeal of sentences imposed in felony cases in federal district courts. As passed by the Senate in 1967, Senate Bill 1540 allowed an appeal on the grounds that the sentence was excessive and guaranteed that "sentences reflect similarities in the circumstances of defendants prosecuted for the same crimes."[11] Although appellate review of sentences did not become law in the 1960s, this provision surfaced during the next decade as part of a larger effort to recodify federal criminal law.

The seeds of federal criminal code reform were, indeed, sown during this earlier period. In 1966 Congress established a twelve-member National Commission of Reform of Federal Criminal Laws to examine the federal code and to recommend improvements in the criminal justice system. The commission's final report, filed in January of 1971, laid the groundwork for codification of criminal law encompassing offenses, sentences, and procedures. Thus, while the 1960s were colored by a relative lack of concern with limiting discretion in judicial decision making, the period did produce the cornerstone for major activity in the 1970s.

As indicated in Figure 9.1, there was a marked increase during the 1970s in legislative activity designed to limit judicial discretion. The single most significant congressional effort in this area was centered in comprehensive legislation aimed at revising the federal criminal code. After four years of extensive hearings and legislative work, the Senate Judiciary Subcommittee on Criminal Laws and Procedure, chaired by Senator John McClellan, reported to the full committee a bill (Senate Bill 1) designed to codify and reform the federal criminal law. Included in the bill's 750 pages were provisions to create a rational and comprehensive system of sentencing that would guide the use of discretion by the judiciary. In addition, the bill sought to establish a limited system of appellate review of federal criminal sentences in felony cases.

The legislation remained in committee during 1976, but a successor bill, Senate 1437, was reported by the Senate Judiciary Committee in 1977 and passed by the Senate in 1978. Proponents of the Criminal Code Reform Act strongly endorsed the provisions of the bill, which rationalized the definitions of criminal behavior, and they viewed those dealing with sentences as the most far-reaching improvement in the criminal code. Efforts to ensure consistency in punishment included the delineation of specific classes of crimes, the creation of a sentencing commission to promulgate sentencing guidelines for judges, a movement toward more "determinate" sentences, the virtual elimination of parole, and provision for appellate review of sentencing decisions.

A third major attempt to rewrite the federal criminal code came in 1979 with

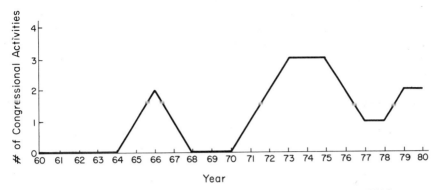

FIG. 9.1.   CONGRESSIONAL ACTIVITIES AIMED AT LIMITING
JUDICIAL DISCRETION.

the report of Senate Bill 1722 by the Senate Judiciary Committee. A similar bill, House of Representatives Bill 6915, was reported by the House Judiciary Committee in 1980. Neither measure was called up for floor action.

While the passage of a federal criminal law reform measure eluded Congress during the 1970s, Congress was successful in revising federal parole procedures to make them more equitable. After five years of work by both the House and Senate judiciary committees, legislation reorganizing the federal parole system became public law in 1976. Viewed by Representative Robert Kastenmeier as "the most important criminal justice legislation of the 94th Congress," the bill reconstituted the U.S. Board of Parole as the U.S. Parole Commission and was intended to replace arbitrary parole procedures with clear standards and safeguards. The wide range of discretion exercised by parole boards had come under increased attack by wardens, prisoners, and judges. The new legislation limited the discretionary power of the boards by shifting the burden of proof for determining the suitability for parole from the prisoner to the parole board. In addition, the bill set standards for assuring that parole decision would be openly reached by a fair and reasonable process.

During this time Congress also asserted its power vis-à-vis the judiciary by enacting a uniform code of evidence for use in federal courts. As passed by Congress in 1974 and signed into law the next year, the bill (House of Representatives Bill 5463) codified the types of evidence that could and could not be used in federal courts and thus sought to bring some consistency to the evidential decisions made by trial court judges.

Congress took similar action in 1975 to revise the Federal Rules of Criminal Procedure. Among the provisions that became public law was one giving formal recognition to the propriety of plea bargaining. As adopted, Rule 11 structured the discretion exercised in plea negotiations and was aimed at bringing uniformity to plea-bargaining procedures.

Hints of congressional desire to limit the exercise of discretion in certain decision-making situations can be found in three additional pieces of legislation considered by Congress in recent years. In the Omnibus Crime Control and Safe Streets Act Amendments of 1973, for example, the Senate included mandatory jail sentences for drug pushers and for persons committing felonies while possessing a firearm. Here legislative activity was directed toward limiting discretion in sentencing in specific kinds of cases. By requiring the dismissal of charges against a person not brought to trial within 100 days of arrest, Congress in 1974 also sought to impose more structure on judicial decisions regarding trial schedules.[12] Finally, congressional effort during 1980 was directed toward expanding demonstration programs designed to help federal judges make pretrial bail decisions. Originally established in 1974 as part of the Speedy Trial Act, the programs provided federal judges with pretrial services to guide their decision making.

This examination of congressional activity suggests that Congress did relatively little to reduce discretion in the federal criminal justice system during the twenty year period under study. Clearly, more congressional effort was directed toward limiting discretion in the 1970s than in the previous decade, but fully one half of the legislative "activities" that occurred between 1970 and 1980 were concerned with the single issue of reforming the federal criminal code. Congress was not successful in enacting this comprehensive legislation; those bills that did become public law represent only piecemeal efforts to structure discretionary decision making at critical stages of the criminal justice process. Given the concern that many, both within and outside the legislature, have expressed over the lack of consistency and the abuses of discretion in the justice system, why has Congress done so little to reduce discretion and structure its use?

EXPLAINING CONGRESSIONAL FAILURE

Much of the recent research concerned with legislative behavior speaks to the reelection goal of members of the U.S. Congress. In his seminal work, Mayhew suggests that members of Congress might be viewed as "single-minded seekers of reelection."[13] Toward this end, legislators undertake advertising, credit-claiming, and position-taking activities. Advertising is described as "attempts to disseminate one's name among constituents"; credit claiming is defined as fostering "the belief that the relevant political actor is personally responsible for causing the government to do something desirable." In the congressional setting, this activity generally falls under the broad category of casework. Finally, position taking refers to making a "statement on anything of interest to political actors." It is Mayhew's contention that legislators perform all these activities with the aim of getting reelected.

In a similar vein, Fiorina suggests that legislators are typically engaged in a "mix of three kinds of activities: lawmaking, pork barreling, and casework."[14] What is perhaps most relevant for this discussion is his claim that casework takes up as much time as the other two activities put together. Fiorina claims, "What should we expect from a legislative body composed of individuals whose first priority is continued tenure in office? We should expect [to find that the] normal activities of its members are those calculated to enhance their chances of reelection." Hence, like Mayhew, Fiorina is suggesting that most congressional behavior is directed toward the reelection goal.

Toward this aim of reelection, members are prone to exploit the benefits of congressional office. As Cover notes, "Incumbents have access to a variety of politically useful perquisites and there is evidence suggesting that these 'perqs' have been used to sway votes."[15] Moreover, he says, members of Congress who are relatively "unsafe and unsenior" have a propensity to exploit perquisites that assist them in keeping close contact with their districts.

Parker speaks to increases in use of perquisites as well, but he also is concerned with increases in district attentiveness. He found increases in trips back to the district by both junior and senior members of the House and concluded that the increases in district attention appear to be a function of both greater travel allotments and the behavior of recently elected members.[16] Parker suggests two implications of his findings that should be mentioned. First, like others who have examined the benefits and behavior of incumbent members of Congress, he claims that it will be increasingly difficult to unseat them. Second, Parker expects that increased district attentiveness found in his research might enhance a legislator's flexibility in voting. That is to suggest that having successfully "serviced" the district, the legislator will be free to exercise his or her own judgment in the actual law-making function.

Parker's findings seem to present a paradox that provides an excellent springboard for discussion of why Congress has been relatively unsuccessful in producing legislation limiting judicial discretion. On the one hand, as current research suggests, legislators engage in the kinds of activities that will enhance their own reelection. Therefore, it might be argued that devoting one's time to legislation that will provide no one with tangible benefits is not in the best interest of the election-minded Congressperson. This may explain why Congress has done so little in the area of limiting judicial discretion; the reelection "payoff" is simply not that great. On the other hand, casework and attentiveness (for example, trips to the district) may free the legislator to work his or her own will in a policy sense. Thus, we might assume that legislation such as that which limits judicial discretion could be ripe for some of the now "freed" representatives' time.[17]

Are relevant members now feeling sufficiently "free" to engage in such legislative activity? The answer to this question may be found, in part, by looking at the goals of members of the judiciary committees in Congress. In a study of the House Judiciary Committee, Lynette Perkins found that there were more members with the primary goal of reelection than there were with the goal of formulating "good public policy." Perkins views this as surprising because the "activist reputation of former Chairman Emanuel Celler and the Judiciary Committee's jurisdiction seemed to indicate that members with policy orientations would predominate.[18] In effect, then, Perkins is suggesting that among the members of the Judiciary Committee in the House there is concern with reelection significant enough to have an impact on the policy orientation of the committee.

Perkins also notes that changes in the overall complexion of the committee have had an effect on the policy activities of the committee's members. She argues that the prestige of the Judiciary Committee has suffered as a result of the change in the chair from Celler to Peter Rodino, claiming that prestige was greater under the policy activist Celler than is the case under the more reelection minded Rodino. Furthermore, when prestige was greater, members with strong reelection goals did not seek membership on the Judiciary Committee because it was not seen as a place where those goals would be enhanced. In point of fact, Perkins suggests that the prestige and policy orientation of the committee were paramount in its ability to attract freshmen members. With the loss of prestige, the major attraction of the committee has diminished as well.

It appears as though the Parker argument, that insured relection will allow freedom in policymaking activity, is not particularly relevant for the case of congressional activity and limiting judicial discretion. Perkins' research leads to this conclusion on two grounds; first, in the case of the House Judiciary Committee at least, members are not yet sufficiently safe (so far as they are concerned) to devote much time to the writing and passage of this type of legislation. Second, the orientation of the committee membership seems to be moving in a direction opposite to that predicted by Parker. Rather than seeing a stronger policy orientation, we are finding a greater reelection orientation on the part of the members of the Judiciary Committee. This might suggest that recent findings regarding the goals of legislators indicate that drafting legislation seeking to limit discretion is a low-priority task. Simply stated, relatively little activity of this kind is undertaken because it may not be perceived as enhancing a representative's chances for reelection.

A second, though related, explanation for the dearth of congressional action to structure the exercise of discretion in the criminal justice process lies in the nature of the task itself. In many respects, legislative attempts to limit judicial discretion are similar to oversight activity. Hence, those factors that generally work against successful performance of the oversight function also may be contributing to the relative lack of congressional activity in this area.

Congress has the legal responsibility to oversee the activities of the federal bureaucracy. In fact, the Legislative Reorganization Act of 1946 states that each standing committee will "exercise continuous watchfulness of the execution by the administrative agencies concerned of any laws, the subject matter of which is within the jurisdiction of such committee." More recently, in the Subcommittee Bill of Rights adopted in the early 1970s by the Democratic congressional caucus, it was established that each standing committee with a membership of twenty or greater should have at least four subcommittees, one of which is to be formed for the express purpose of oversight. This indeed suggests a recognition on the part of Congress that systematic oversight ought to be conducted.

As defined by Morris Ogul, *oversight* is the "behavior by legislators and their staffs, individually or collectively, which results in an impact, intended or not, on bureaucratic behavior."[19] Limitations placed on the amount of discretion that can be exercised by judicial officers fit neatly into this definition of legislative activity having an impact on bureaucratic behavior. Whether one wishes to claim that the potentially affected judicial officers are or are not bureaucrats is really a question of semantics. Moreover, there is an obvious parallel between legislation that specifically seeks to limit discretion (as oversight) and more "typical" oversight, which seeks to establish whether congressional intent of a program is being met by the actions of the implementing agency. Simply put, each of these activities would affect the way other governmental actors discharge their responsibilities.

Assuming the similarity between the type of legislation discussed in this chapter and other types of oversight activities, we might examine the factors that influence successful performance of oversight. Ogul suggests that oversight is most likely to occur when the following characteristics, among others, are present: "a legal basis for committee or individual activity;...subject matter that is not unusually technical or complex enough to require special expertise;...activities involved that are centralized in one executive department;...an issue with high visibility and large political payoffs;...a member's strong interest in the work of his committee and the particular subject matter at hand...."[20] Ogul suggests that while the presence of these factors will maximize the possibilities for oversight, their absence will minimize those possibilities.

Ogul's prescriptions for successful oversight do not seem to bode well for the possibility of legislating the amount of discretion to be exercised in judicial decision making. While the judiciary committees clearly have the authority to oversee the amount of discretion used (in Ogul's terms, they have the "legal basis"), chances for success are still minimal. This substantive area encompasses complex and technical issues. Furthermore, discretionary decisions are not centralized in one agency or department; rather, they occur at many critical stages of the criminal justice process.

The final points in Ogul's prescriptions for successful oversight lead back to earlier speculations as to why Congress has been relatively unsuccessful in this area. Members of Congress will engage in activities that are high in visibility and political payoffs. Such activities usually fall within the purview of constituent casework, rather than in legislating technical and specialized issues. In addition, oversight activity in general is viewed as a low-priority task. Most question the political payoffs of oversight, suggesting that those payoffs are most often negligible. As Lees notes, "Political payoffs may be more critical than either the complexity or visibility of issues or information resources and committee structures."[21]

In summary, between 1960 and 1980 Congress did little to limit or structure the exercise of discretion in the federal criminal justice system. Despite widespread concern over the abuses of discretionary decision making, congressional response has been piecemeal at best. One impediment to reform has been the behavioral motivations of legislators. There are few political benefits to be had from expending much effort on this kind of activity, which, we have noted, is not unlike legislative oversight. In addition, the incremental processes that characterize congressional policymaking do not lend themselves to comprehensive revisions of complex laws. Moreover, any attempts to bring about comprehensive change are met with divisive controversy, thereby limiting chances for success. The dynamics of the legislative process, therefore, go a long way toward explaining congressional failure to enact much legislation designed to limit judicial discretion.

Somewhat paradoxically, it may be the internal dynamics of the criminal justice system that provide the most realistic limitations on discretionary decision making. In response to conflicting demands and varying conceptions of justice, those involved in processing criminal cases operate on the basis of shared norms and develop standards that structure discretion. Narrowing the range of discretion that is exercised remains an important goal. Efforts to achieve consistency, however, must be undertaken with the recognition of the dynamics of the process and a realistic assessment of the chances for success.

CHAPTER TEN

Mediation as an Alternative to Civil Rights Litigation

RICHARD A. SALEM

IN MAY 1979 the Community Relations Service (CRS) of the U.S. Department of Justice embarked on a pilot project with district judges in the Seventh Federal Circuit (Illinois, Indiana, and Wisconsin) to determine the viability and value of mediation as an alternative to litigation in civil rights cases. During the thirty ensuing months, CRS received from the courts twenty-six referrals in the areas of employment, housing, corrections, community involvement, and voting rights. A review of the results of those cases, combined with feedback from judges, magistrates, the parties, and their counsel, indicate that through formal mediation CRS can help resolve complex civil rights cases to the satisfaction of the parties more quickly and at a substantially lower cost than what otherwise would have been possible. While pretrial settlements represent a commonly used technique in civil cases, there is evidence that the judges and magistrates actually held out little expectation of pretrial settlements in a number of the cases successfully resolved by CRS. Further, there are signs that the mediation process raised the parties' expectations that future civil rights complaints might be resolved through negotiations without the need for litigation.

CRS AS A DISPUTE RESOLUTION AGENCY

The decision to propose the pilot project to the judiciary was a logical and timely step for the conflict resolution agency. The Community Relations Service has been assisting communities to resolve racial and ethnic disputes since it was established by Congress under Title X of the Civil Rights Act of 1964. Originally a part of the Department of Commerce, CRS was transferred to the Department of Justice in a reorganization of 1966. Unlike most other units in that department, CRS has no law enforcement, compliance, investigative, or litigative authority. Title X even makes it a federal offense for CRS to assist other agencies in investigations or to share information obtained in confidence. This confidentiality clause

Richard A. Salem, School of Law, Loyola University of Chicago, private consultant and former Midwest director of Community Relations Service, U.S. Department of Justice.

has enhanced CRS's abilities to gain the confidence of disputants and bring about negotiated settlements.

While CRS's founding legislation has remained basically the same since the agency's inception, the techniques used by its staff have changed over the years to accommodate the changing patterns of civil rights protest.

Early in its history the primary concern of CRS was helping communities resolve civil rights disputes that had the potential to develop into violent confrontations. The CRS conciliator's traditional role was to attempt to establish rapport and develop a working relationship with each of the parties. The conciliator would attempt to open lines of communication between the disputants, often serving as a liaison between them and helping to interpret developments so that each side could better understand the other's needs. The conciliator would help the parties identify resources and options that could contribute to a prompt and peaceful resolution of the conflict. At times, CRS would propose settlements to the parties, but the agency came to learn that the most enduring agreements were the ones struck by the parties themselves.

In the late 1960s and early 1970s the nature of civil rights protests began to change from spontaneous outbursts and massive demonstrations to more controlled protests and bills of particulars specifying the forms of relief that were demanded and expected. Protest moved from the streets to the negotiating table. The Community Relations Service responded by training its field staff—already skilled as conciliators—in formal mediation, a process of negotiation and compromise. After employing techniques of conciliation to ease tensions by opening communications between the parties and clarifying interests and issues, CRS might propose that the underlying dispute be resolved through formal mediation. When successful, the result would be a signed agreement drawn up by the parties with the help of the CRS mediator. It was a totally voluntary process. Many racial conflicts involving employment, education, corrections, or police-community issues were resolved in this manner. It was clear to CRS, and often to the parties, that many of the negotiated settlements brought about with the assistance of CRS mediators resolved matters that otherwise would have ended up in federal courts.

In 1973 CRS mediated its first case for the federal judiciary at the request of U.S. District Judge E. Gordon West, of the Middle District of Louisiana, in the Fifth Circuit. It was a civil rights complaint filed by black inmates against officials at the State Prison in Angola, Louisiana. Mediator Robert Greenwald brought the parties together on twenty-eight issues.

During the next six years, federal judges called upon CRS on an ad hoc basis to mediate, conciliate, fact find, or provide technical assistance in two dozen cases, predominantly in the areas of corrections and education. In eleven of these cases, judges issued orders instructing CRS to help communities minimize racial conflict during the start up of court-ordered school desegregation.

Use of CRS by the judiciary was anticipated by the agency's creators. Title II of the Civil Rights Act of 1964 permits a judge to refer a public accommodations case to CRS for up to sixty days in an effort to bring about a voluntary resolution of the matter. Despite the interest in CRS by the judiciary, however, there is no record of a judge having called upon the agency to resolve a Title II dispute.

INTEREST IN MEDIATION IN THE SEVENTH FEDERAL CIRCUIT

The use of formal mediation to assist district judges in the Seventh Federal Circuit on a regular basis was first suggested in 1978 by a circuit subcommittee on alternatives to litigation.[1] A two-year pilot project was proposed that would utilize CRS for civil rights cases, the Federal Mediation and Conciliation Service for labor cases, and the American Arbitration Association for cases that fell outside the jurisdiction of the other two agencies. When it became apparent that it would take at least two years for the circuit to complete consideration of the recommendation, CRS's Midwest Regional Office proposed a separate project with the court. In a panel presentation at the annual Seventh Circuit conference on May 9, 1979, CRS Director Gilbert G. Pompa invited the district judges to draw on the agency's experience in resolving civil rights disputes. The first case was referred the following morning.

The prompt and positive response from the judges to CRS's offer to mediate did not come as a surprise. Settling civil cases without going to trial is an integral part of the judicial process and an important discretionary tool for both judges and the parties. Faced with heavy backlogs and potentially long and expensive trials, judges traditionally help bring parties to pretrial settlements. While some judges are viewed as passive in this role, others press hard for negotiated settlements in civil cases and will function as mediators to enhance the process.

The role of district judges in the settlement process was explored at a seminar for newly appointed judges conducted by the Federal Judicial Center in 1973. As the resulting report noted, "The seminar concluded that the judge has a role that assumes much greater force for all participants in the settlement process. Not only do judges themselves have responsibility, but lawyers expect and indeed in many instances feel it is necessary for the judge to be actively involved as a mediator."[2]

Interest in the availability of CRS mediators might have been heightened by the large number of civil rights and corrections complaints filed in the Seventh Circuit. Those two categories accounted for more than 26 percent (2,147 complaints) of all civil complaints filed in the seven-district circuit during the two years of 1976–1977, according to figures compiled by the circuit staff.

CASES REFERRED TO CRS

Corrections. The first referral to come out of the pilot project was from Senior Judge Hubert L. Will. The focus was a 1976 Civil Rights Division complaint that race was the determining factor in the assignment of inmates to housing units at Cook County Jail in Chicago. Mediator Jesse Taylor brought the parties to a settlement following several negotiating sessions over a period of six months.

Two months later, U.S. District Judge Myron L. Gordon of the Eastern District of Wisconsin asked CRS to mediate a dispute in which inmates at the state prison in Waupun alleged discrimination in the treatment of blacks in the prison's adjustment center. There were numerous issues, including food, heat, recreation time, visiting privileges, and the use of Mace to quell unruly inmates. The agreement brought about by mediator Werner E. Petterson led to the settlement of all oustanding issues in this case and four others that had been pending. Three other corrections cases were subsequently referred by Judge Gordon; CRS was unable to resolve them.

Voting Rights. Chief Judge James L. Foreman, in the Southern District of Illinois, asked CRS to mediate a class action suit in which voting-age blacks in Cairo, Illinois, contended that the at-large system of electing city commissioners had precluded the election of a black to city office for more than sixty years. Cairo's population is 30–40 percent black. One of the plaintiffs, Ms. Hattie Kendrick, eighty-six years old, contended that she had not had the opportunity to vote for a black candidate for the city commission in her fifty years as a registered voter.

The plaintiffs sought to change the form of government to a city council with aldermen elected from single-member districts. The case, originally filed in 1973, was referred to CRS in October 1979. Mediators Richard A. Salem and Gustavo Gaynett helped the parties reach agreement early the following year. The "mixed aldermanic" government agreed upon resulted in two blacks being elected to the city council the following November.

Employment. A black applicant who had been denied a guard's position at the Cook County Jail in Chicago filed a class action suit in 1978 alleging that lie detector tests used to screen job applicants were racially discriminatory. At the request of Judge Stanley J. Roszkowski, CRS brought the disputants to a settlement that placed severe restrictions on the use of the polygraph and gave minority applicants who previously had been denied jobs for this reason an opportunity to reapply.

In 1974 CRS provided technical assistance to the court and school district in Springfield, Illinois, during the implementation of court-mandated school desegregation in that city. In 1980, at the request of District Judge J. Waldo Ackerman, CRS returned to mediate a dispute that arose when black teachers in the district alleged that the affirmative action provisions of the desegregation order were being violated through the removal of minority teachers who lacked sufficient seniority.

CRS successfully mediated one of three additional employment cases.

Housing. In a highly publicized suit filed in 1979, three Chicago suburban communities alleged racial discrimination through steering by a realtor. At the request of Magistrate Olga Jurco and Judge Nicholas J. Bua, CRS was able to overcome the high level of hostility between the parties and in October 1981 counsel advised the court that they had reached agreement. However, the defendant declined to sign a proposed consent decree until an earlier case that had been brought against the realtor by one of the communities was resolved. (The court promptly assigned that case to CRS and it was subsequently resolved through mediation.)

In an unusual action in 1980, Judge Hubert L. Will asked CRS to mediate a case that had already been tried. Elected officials in Du Page County, Illinois, were charged in 1971 with illegally blocking federally subsidized low-income housing in the county. Judge Will called the parties, their counsels, and CRS into his chambers in May 1980 after the trial and advised them that before releasing his decision he wanted to try to obtain a voluntary settlement. He said he was trying to avoid the costly and lengthy appeals, which he viewed as inevitable no matter how he ruled. CRS was unable to bring the parties to mediation, and the judge later ruled for the plaintiffs. Within hours of the decision the defendants announced they would appeal.

CRS also mediated two other cases in which owners of apartment projects were accused of racial discrimination and one a case in which the city of Joliet, Illinois, was accused of blocking low-income housing. In one other housing case, CRS was unable to bring about final resolution of a suit to force the city of Chicago and the Department of Housing and Urban Development to provide subsidized housing for low-income residents of the Uptown community who were threatened with removal by new real estate development.

Community Involvement. In one of the first cases referred to CRS, a broad-based coalition of minority and low-income groups in Chicago alleged that the city of Chicago and the U.S. Economic Development Administration failed to give minorities and low-income residents an adequate voice in the Chicago Overall Economic Development Plan (OEDP). The CRS brought the parties to an agreement under which twelve individuals nominated by community organizations representing the plaintiff class would be designated to serve on the OEDP advisory body mandated under federal law.

Magistrate Jurco asked CRS in November 1981 to mediate a complaint alleging that the Chicago Park District was discriminating in the allocation of resources to black residents of the Chicago neighborhoods served by the plaintiff, the Midwest Community Council. Mediation was unsuccessful and the defendant was subsequently acquitted.

Mediation of another community involvement case was terminated when the court of appeals determined that the matter should be handled by the state courts. A final case in which parents of several elementary school children alleged their children had been strip-searched by police and school officials after a teacher's wallet was found to be missing, was returned to the court when the parties declined to mediate.

RESULTS OF CRS MEDIATION

Of the twenty-six cases referred to CRS, fifteen were fully resolved, including five prison complaints that were settled by a single mediated agreement. In two of the twenty-six cases the parties advised the court that they had reached a mediated agreement but final settlement wasn't achieved; the cases were returned to the court. Eight were returned to the court because CRS was unable to bring the parties to the table. In another case, mediation was terminated when the court of appeals ruled that the matter should be handled by the state courts.

Because CRS wanted to encourage the referral of cases from judges under this demonstration project, all requests for CRS involvement were honored; no cases were declined. A close look at the results, however, suggests that the screening of referrals could substantially increase the success rate. For example:

— Thirteen of the fifteen cases settled through mediation were either class action suits or actions brought by community organizations or three or more individuals.

— Five of the eight matters in which the mediator was unable to bring the parties to the table involved cases with very limited impact. Two were individual employment cases that came to the court and CRS after the Equal Employment Opportunity Commission had been unable to obtain a settlement; one of those cases was subsequently dismissed when the plaintiff failed to appear in court as ordered. Three others were inmate cases involving only the plaintiffs and not the general inmate populations.

— Mediation was stymied in two cases involving political jurisdictions accused of closing their communities to federally subsidized low-income housing. Elected officials with conservative constituencies were not amenable to a negotiated settlement, even though it apeared they anticipated losing their cases in court at considerable cost in legal fees. Federally subsidized low-income housing might come to their communities by court order, but preferably not through a voluntary agreement. This response was consistent with CRS's experience in dealing with elected officials in sensitive school desegregation cases and other cases over the years.

The value of using outside mediators to bring about settlements in cases that didn't originally appear amenable to pretrial resolution was reflected in statements made in court and in follow-up correspondence by judges, magistrates, and counsel. There are a number of examples:

— Upon being advised that agreement had been reached in the Cook County Jail segregation case, Judge Will described it as "a pretty remarkable achievement considering when the case first started everybody said 'never, never, never will this case be resolved short of trial.' " When he entered the consent decree on January 4, 1980, he called it "really a tribute to the effectiveness of the Community Relations Service . . . which has resolved this lawsuit which I thought was going to take me a great deal of time and effort to resolve."

— Magistrate Jurco expressed her "deep appreciation" in a letter to CRS commenting on the mediator's ability in the racial "steering" case to bring the parties to agreement: "When the Community Relations Service, at the request of Judge Bua, entered the matter to negotiate with the parties with a view to resolution of this litigation, it appeared an almost impossible task because of strong personal opinions of the litigants."

— Bitterness between the parties was even more evident in the voting rights case in Cairo where there had been a long history of racial conflict. "When the signed agreement was presented to Judge Foreman on March 11, 1980, defense attorney John Feirich told the court the "contribution of CRS to the settlement of this case was monumental, and that's an understatement. It would not have been reached without their efforts, I feel certain."

The CRS's success in these cases probably was attributable to the agency's long years of experience in dealing with volatile disputes. Also important was its persistence in leading the parties to a settlement despite a high level of rhetoric that might discourage neutrals not familiar with the dynamics of community conflict resolution.

The significance of a settlement reached by the disputants over one imposed by a judge was emphasized by plaintiff attorney Harvey Grossman in the Cairo case when he told the court, "I think the defendants and the named plaintiffs have reached a settlement which is geared toward establishing racial harmony in a town that has been torn by racial strife historically, and we are hopeful that the propositions on which this case has been settled will have a result that is far superior than anything mandated or forced on a litigant. The settlement should be approved with a view towards allowing people to resolve conflicts by way of negotiations rather than imposition of court order."

A similar response came from plaintiffs in the suit in which minorities and low-income people sought a voice in the Chicago Overall Economic Development Plan. One veteran black leader was quoted in June 1980 by the Chicago Sun-Times as saying, "I can remember when all we could do was stand out on the street and picket and scream.... We didn't get all we asked for, but we got [the settlement] and we are satisfied." Another plaintiff added: "All that time we couldn't even get the city to talk to us. CRS got us to the table. So we feel this has opened the process to the people."

These assessments may be overly optimistic; it is by no means clear from the limited experience of this project that reaching out-of-court settlements in civil rights cases will make it easier for the parties to resolve future disputes. Nonetheless, the optimism is consistent with the theory underlying the pilot project, that there are distinct advantages to a solution developed by the parties over one imposed by the court. For example:

— Mediation requires the parties to hear each other's views, something CRS over the years has found doesn't occur prior to litigation in a large number of cases.

— In a confidential mediation session, the parties and their counsel can deal with perceptions, emotions, and even hard facts that would not be admissible in the courtroom. Mediation can deal with the history of a conflict, something the court would be unable to take into consideration. Also, the pattern of dialogue and negotiation established during mediation helps ease tensions and obviate the bitterness that often follows court-imposed solutions.

— CRS experience over the years suggests that mediated settlements increase the likelihood that the parties will be able to resolve future disputes without the need for outside intervention.

Comments from the judge and the parties substantiated another underlying premise of the pilot project: substantial savings in both time and money can be achieved through mediation as an alternative to litigation. Had the Cairo voting rights case gone to trial, it would have taken up to three years to fully resolve at a cost of hundreds of thousands of dollars to the parties, according to estimates from the judge and the counsel. The Joliet housing case has been costing the city approximately $100,000 a year in legal expenses during the pretrial stage, and if the matter goes to trial the judicial process is expected to last an additional five years, according to an estimate by the magistrate who assigned the case to CRS. Had CRS not intervened in the Cook County Jail segregation case, the cost to taxpayers would have been approximately fifty thousand dollars in lawyer and court expenses, according to a preliminary evaluation of the pilot project by CRS.[3]

While it is assumed that a continuing program of mediation would result in some dollar savings to the judiciary, it isn't clear from this project how extensive those savings would be or whether such a program could significantly affect court backlogs. Nonetheless, the preliminary evaluation by CRS indicates that a conservative estimate of dollar savings in cases brought to resolution by CRS far exceeds the cost of the mediation.

Based on the initial results of the pilot project, former Attorney General Benjamin R. Civiletti authorized a CRS increase in its field staff by more than 10 percent (ten positions) to provide mediators to handle an increased workload from the federal judiciary. In his fiscal year 1982 budget policy guidelines to Department of Justice managers, he said CRS mediation as an alternative to litigation "is expected to reduce government costs by decreasing the case loads of individual judges and the need for additional court administrative support staff and has received acclaim from the federal judiciary as a result of its initial success."

The former attorney general's enthusiasm notwithstanding, budget cuts proposed after the presidential election of November 1980 canceled the proposed staff increase even before Mr. Civiletti departed. The CRS continues to offer mediation services to the federal courts, but it never has made another concerted effort to interest judges in mediation and only a few requests for assistance are received from the judiciary.

Summary of Cases Referred for Mediation

CORRECTIONS

Judge Will
Northern District, Illinois
Case 76–C–4768
Assigned to CRS: 05-10-79
Mediator: Taylor

Civil Rights Division, U.S. Dept. of Justice, alleged racial discrimination in the housing of inmates at Cook County Jail, Chicago.

The case was successfully mediated; a consent decree was entered January 4, 1980. The National Institute of Corrections (NIC) would develop a comprehensive inmate classification plan for assigning inmates to housing units in a manner that would not discriminate against or separate inmates on the basis of their race, color or national origin. The agreement also included training and record keeping components. The services of NIC were arranged by CRS at no cost to the parties.

Judge Gordon
Eastern District, Wisconsin
Case 79–C–19
Assigned to CRS: 07–09–79
Mediator: Petterson (Glenn)

Inmates at the Waupun Correctional Institution alleged discrimination in the treatment of blacks in the prison's adjustment center.

The case was successfully mediated; a stipulation was signed February 18, 1980, and the case was dismissed.

Judge Gordon
Eastern District, Wisconsin
Case 79–C–746
Assigned to CRS: 09–25–79
Mediator: Petterson

Inmate at Waupun Correctional Institution filed a complaint raising issues similar to those in Case 79–C–19 above.

The plaintiff asked the court to dismiss the case in light of the settlement of Case 79–C–19, above. Case was dismissed.

Judge Doyle	Inmates at Waupun Correctional Institution
Western District, Wisconsin	who were plaintiffs in Case 79–C–19, above,
Case 78–C–291	filed similar complaints in Western District of
Case 78–C–328	Wisconsin.
Case 78–C–358	
Assigned to CRS: 07–13–79	
Mediator: Petterson	

Plaintiffs advised the court that stipulation signed in Case 79–C–19 (Eastern District), above, resolved their complaints. Case was dismissed.

Judge Gordon	Inmate alleged racial discrimination in disci-
Eastern District, Wisconsin	plinary action in adjustment center at Waupun
Case 80–C–964	Correctional Institution.
Assigned to CRS: 10–28–80	
Mediator: Petterson	

Mediation did not produce agreement. Case returned to court.

Judge Gordon	Inmates at Correctional Institution, Green Bay,
Eastern District, Wisconsin	Wisconsin, alleged undue restrictions while un-
Case 79–C–885	der protective custody.
Assigned to CRS: 01–30–80	
Mediator: Petterson	

Inmates were due for transfer and advised CRS they wanted to drop complaint. Case returned to court.

Judge Gordon	Plaintiff alleged racial discrimination in inmate
Eastern District, Wisconsin	pay scale at Fox Lake Correctional Institution.
Case 79–C–591	
Assigned to CRS: 04–21–80	
Mediator: Petterson	

One party declined to mediate. Case returned to court.

EMPLOYMENT

Judge Roszkowski	Job applicant at Cook County Jail, Chicago,
Northern District, Illinois	alleged racial discrimination in the use of lie
Case 78–C–1572	detector for hiring of correctional guards.
Assigned to CRS: 03–20–80	
Mediator: Petterson	

Case successfully mediated; it was agreed that restrictions would be placed on the use of polygraph testing. All minority applicants who had been denied jobs on the basis of polygraph testing would be contacted and offered an opportunity to reapply.

Judge Ackerman	Black staff members in the Springfield, Illinois,
Central District, Illinois	school system alleged that the affirmative action
Case 74–C–44	provisions of a school desegregation case court
Assigned to CRS: 04–28–80	order were being violated through the firing of
Mediator: Petterson	minority teachers who lacked sufficient senior-
	ity.

Case successfully mediated; school officials and plaintiffs agreed that minority teachers who had been laid off would be rehired to fill available vacancies. The agreement also provided job protection for minority teachers who lacked sufficient seniority.

Judge Flaum
Northern District, Illinois
Case 79-C-1329
Assigned to CRS: 08-27-80

Hispanic plaintiff alleged racial discrimination in hiring by Maywood, Illinois, Police Department.

Case successfully mediated. Settlement was financial.

Judge McMillen
Northern District, Illinois
Case 79-C-4256
Assigned to CRS: 05-28-80
Mediator: McKinney

Former faculty member alleged reverse discrimination in his removal from Chicago State University.

CRS unable to bring the parties to mediation. Case returned to court.

Judge McMillen
Northern District, Illinois
Case 79-C-4578
Assigned to CRS: 06-10-80
Mediator: McKinney

Individual charged racial discrimination in firing by carpet retailer.

CRS unable to bring parties to mediation. Case returned to court.

VOTING RIGHTS

Judge Foreman
Southern District, Illinois
Case 73-C-19
Assigned to CRS: 10-11-79
Mediators: Salem, Gaynett

Black voters in Cairo, Illinois, sought to replace at-large elected city commission with aldermanic city council elected by wards.

Case successfully mediated. Consent decree entered March 11, 1980. Parties agreed to a city council with five members elected from single-member districts and one council member and the mayor elected at large. Two of the districts were predominantly black.

HOUSING

Judge Roszkowski
Northern District, Illinois
Case 79-C-989
Assigned to CRS: 03-03-80
Mediator: Taylor

Residents of predominantly black, HUD-subsidized Indian Trails Apartments, Chicago, alleged deterioration of services since 1975, when project was 94% white. Case partially resolved in court prior to assignment to CRS.

Remaining issues successfully mediated. Consent decree entered March 1, 1981. Agreement addressed maintenance and repairs to be completed, use of federal rent subsidies, and financial settlement.

Judge Bua/Magistrate Jurco
Northern District, Illinois
Case 79-C-4091
Assigned to CRS: 05-06-80
Mediator: Petterson

Chicago suburban communities of Hazel Crest, Glenwood, and Country Club Hills alleged racial discrimination (steering) in real estate sales by Arquilla-De Haan Realtors.

Case successfully mediated.

Judges Marshall, Bua
Northern District, Illinois
Case 75-C-1231
Assigned to CRS: 10-23-81
Mediator: Peterson

Community of Hazel Crest, Illinois, alleged racial discrimination in housing sales by Arquilla-De Haan Realtors.

Case successfully mediated.

Judge McMillen
Northern District, Illinois
Case 80-C-4612
Assigned to CRS: 10-22-80
Mediator: Petterson

Fair housing organization representing Hispanics alleged racial discrimination in tenant selection at 300-unit Aspen Ridge Apartments in West Chicago, Illinois.

Case successfully mediated.

Judge Will
Northern District, Illinois
Case 71-C-5187
Assigned to CRS: 05-16-80
Mediator: Taylor

Fair housing organization alleged public officials of Du Page County, Illinois, blocked federally subsidized low-income housing in the county. Case assigned to CRS after conclusion of trial, but before issuance of court order.

One party declined to mediate. Case returned to court.

Judge Bua/Magistrate Cooley
Northern District, Illinois
Case 75-C-4002
Assigned to CRS: 06-26-79
Mediator: Taylor

Contractor alleged city of Joliet illegally denied building permits for low-income and elderly housing.

Mediation did not produce an agreement.

Judge Crowley
Northern District, Illinois
Assigned to CRS: 03-14-80
Mediator: Taylor

Community organization in Uptown neighborhood of Chicago sought to have the city and HUD adopt a program to provide subsidized housing for residents threatened with being forced out of the community by new real estate development.

Counsel for all parties advised court they had reached a mediated settlement, but city of Chicago ultimately withdrew and declined signing or further mediation.

COMMUNITY INVOLVEMENT

Judge Bua/Magistrate Balog
Northern District, Wisconsin
Case 77-C-2274
Assigned to CRS: 09-27-79
Mediator: Taylor

Community coalition alleged in suit against city of Chicago and U.S. Economic Development Administration that city failed to give low-income and minority residents an adequate voice in Chicago Overall Economic Development Plan.

Case successfully mediated. Consent decree entered July 14, 1980. Parties agreed to a formula to select representatives from plaintiff class to serve on OEDP advisory board.

Judge Roszkowski
Northern District, Illinois
Case 80-C-32
Assigned to CRS: 01-31-80
Mediator: Taylor

Community organization in Uptown area of Chicago sought to prevent cutoff in funding of neighborhood health clinic by Cook County commissioners.

Mediation initiated, then terminated. Seventh Circuit Court of Appeals ruled that the matter should be considered by the state courts.

Judge Leighton/Magistrate Jurco
Northern District, Illinois
Case 79-C-3187
Assigned to CRS: 12-03-81
Mediator: Petterson

Community organization alleged in suit against Chicago Park District that distribution of resources in city parks is racially discriminatory.

CRS unable to bring the parties to mediation.

Judge Marovitz	Parents alleged strip search of their children by
Northern District, Illinois	school officials and police in Chicago elemen-
Case 80-C-246	tary school.
Assigned to CRS: 03-19-80	
Mediator: Petterson	

One party declined mediation. Case returned to court.

CHAPTER ELEVEN

Discretionary Justice at DOJ: Implementing Section 5 of the Voting Rights Act

HOWARD BALL, DALE KRANE, and THOMAS P. LAUTH

THIS CHAPTER is about the exercise of administrative discretion in the enforcement of Section 5 of the 1965 Voting Rights Act (VRA). In an effort to prevent the dilution of black voting strength, Section 5 requires jurisdictions covered by the act to obtain "preclearance" before any changes in voting qualifications, practices, or procedures can be enforced. The inclusion of such a section was designed primarily to prevent the substitution of new discriminatory practices for old ones that previously had been eliminated. Preclearance submissions are examined by administrators in the Voting Section of the Civil Rights Division (CRD) at the U.S. Department of Justice (DOJ) to determine if they have a discriminatory purpose or effect. Two very important aspects of the administrative implementation of this section of the act are (1) obtaining compliance by covered jurisdictions and (2) interpreting the meaning of "discriminatory purpose and effect." In both instances DOJ officials have broad discretion.

This chapter discusses the nature and purpose of discretion, as well as its principal advantages and disadvantages; summarizes the importance of Section 5 for attaining and maintaining minority voting rights; discusses the factors and forces that led to the formulation of administrative regulations governing preclearance submissions; discusses the practices and procedures used by the CRD Voting Section to review Section 5 preclearance submissions; and draws upon evidence to determine the extent to which the administration of Section 5 conforms to a proposed assessment standard.

The authors wish to thank F. Glenn Abney, Georgia State University, for his contribution to the analytical framework used in this chapter.

Howard Ball, Dean, College of Social and Behavioral Sciences, University of Utah, Salt Lake City.
Dale Krane, Mississippi State University, Mississippi State.
Thomas P. Lauth, University of Georgia, Athens.

ADMINISTRATIVE DISCRETION

Public administration is in large measure the governmental process through which broadly articulated social rules are applied to specific sets of circumstances. In this conversion process administrators frequently exercise discretion. In the broad context, discretion is exercised in interpreting legislative intent and applying it to particular situations; in a narrower context, discretion may involve the application and interpretation of agency rules and regulations. Whenever general legislative policy statements are transformed into relatively specific and concrete guides for decisions (known as rules), administrative discretion is limited and standards are set against which official decisions may be compared. Nevertheless, public officials generally retain discretion so long as they are free to make choices from among alternative courses of action or inaction. In Rourke's language, discretion is "the ability of an administrator to choose alternatives—to decide how the power of the state should be used in specific cases."[1]

Administrative discretion is, of course, inevitable because it is virtually impossible (and probably undesirable) for the legislature to enact policies in such detail as to accommodate the wide variety of circumstances likely to emerge in their implementation. Indeed, the capacity of the legislature to forge consensus on important policy questions often is facilitated by agreements to delegate to administrators the responsibility for making judgments about specific policy applications.

For the individual administrator, discretion means flexibility to accommodate unforeseen situations and the ability to individualize policy applications to meet the needs of particular clients or constituencies. Discretion gives administrators both a creative and a reactive capacity to deal with the problems of a complex society.

However, discretion also may mean opportunities for malfeasance or nonfeasance in the form of selective enforcement, prejudice, or favoritism in enforcement. Even when administrators are well-intentioned broad discretionary authority provides the opportunity for administrative interpretations that may alter significantly the intent of official policies. Finally, decisions based upon broad discretionary authority frequently place clients or constituents in the position of not knowing the criteria by which decisions affecting them were made.

The exercise of administrative discretion is important for the implementation of public policy objectives; indeed, it is difficult to imagine policy implementation without the functioning of administrative discretion. Unless discretion on the part of those officials who are three times removed from direct popular control is effectively limited by the rule of law, however, arbitrary and irresponsible actions may result. Since discretion is, as Jowell puts it, "rarely absolute and rarely absent" in administrative decision-making, the important concern is one of balance—reconciling the need and desirability of administrative discretion with the requirement that administrative decisions be subject to the rule of law.[2]

Kenneth Culp Davis has argued that the problem with discretion in the United States is that much administrative activity not now governed by rules should be.[3] He holds that in addition to other safeguards (for example, judicial review), administrative actions also should be subject to predetermined or prospective rules known in advance to the affected parties (covered jurisdictions, for example, as well as administrative decision makers themselves). Davis offers two explanations for the absence of rule-controlled administration: first, the difficulty of formulating rules appropriate to the subject; and second, the preference for discretion over any rules that might be formulated (a belief that discretionary justice produces better results). While a case can be made that "excessive legalization" of administrative decision making may make it difficult for officials to carry out the intent of policies, Davis is of the opinion that the more affected parties know about an agency's laws and policies, the fairer the system.

Theodore J. Lowi has advocated a position similar to that of Davis. Lowi contends that "statutes without standards, policy without law will yield pluralism and bargaining in the system — just as Political Science predicts and pluralism prescribes.[4] If there is to be bargaining, Lowi would prefer the negotiations of "rules" (with the legislature) so as to aggregate and centralize accountability, not negotiation of "decision" (with affected parties), which disaggregates and decentralizes accountability.

Although the Davis-Lowi model of rule-controlled administration may not be the preferred standard, it does serve as a useful benchmark. Against it administrative implementation of Section 5 of the 1965 Voting Rights Act by officials in the Department of Justice can be analyzed.

THE VOTING RIGHTS ACT AND 28 CFR 51

The Voting Rights Act of 1965, as amended in 1970, 1975, and 1982, prohibits through the year 2007 the use of literacy tests and other devices in states where less than 50 percent of the voting age population voted in the November 1964 elections. Examiners from the Department of Justice and observers from the U.S. Civil Service Commission were to be sent to those southern states that fell within the parameters of Section 4 of the act to ensure that black citizens would be registered and allowed to vote. (The southern states originally affected by the 1965 act were Alabama, Georgia, Louisiana, Mississippi, South Carolina, Virginia, and portions of North Carolina.) Although Section 4 suspended several previously used tests and devices because of their discriminatory effect, Section 5 also was enacted to "guard against ingenious actions by those bent on preventing Negroes from voting."[5] It was clearly the intent of the Voting Rights Act to end racial discrimination in voting.

Section 5 effectly froze all voting patterns in the covered jurisdictions as of November 1964 unless the U.S. attorney general of the U.S. district court were to be convinced that the proposed voting change would not dilute black voting strength. It was to be employed to break the cycle of substitution of new discriminatory laws and practices when the old requirements were either suspended or declared unconstitutional. Section 5 requires the covered states to submit any change in "voting qualifications or prerequisites to voting, or standard, practices or procedures with respect to voting" different from that in effect on November 1, 1964, for "preclearance" before any such change can be enforced. Submissions are to be examined to determine if they have either the purpose or effect of denying or abridging the right to vote on account of race or color. The state may seek a declaratory judgment from the Federal Court for the District of Columbia or submit the change to the U.S. attorney general. If the attorney general does not formally object within sixty days, the change may be enforced. Even if the attorney general does object, the state may seek a declaratory judgment from the district court.

Section 5 was included in the Voting Rights Act because of the "acknowledged and anticipated inability of the Justice Department—given limited resources—to investigate independently all changes with respect to voting enacted by states and subdivisions covered by the act."[6] The section placed the burden on covered jurisdictions to submit all voting changes for prior approval. However, the political dynamics of the 1965–1969 era dictated that Section 4—the registration of blacks—had to be the major focus of DOJ activity. James P. Turner, then a staff attorney in the Civil Rights Division, has said "an essential judgment was made that registration was necessary" to break down the southern legal blockade aimed at preventing black voting. Turner estimated that CRD's manpower (about forty lawyers) was committed about 90 percent of the time to Section 4 enforcement, and the remaining 10 percent was devoted to *all* other civil rights problems in the southern section. By the end of the 1960's, according to CRD Voting Section Chief Gerald Jones, the CRD considered its enfranchisement task substantially complete "both by means of federal registration efforts and by the impetus that federal registration had given to local registrars to go ahead and register people." Meanwhile, Section 5 lay dormant, and DOJ policy was to not do anything with that rule, until certain events occurred between 1969 and 1971.

There were a number of events that collectively led the CRD to construct a strategy and elaborate guidelines with respect to Section 5 implementation. These legal, administrative, and political forces had the cumulative effect of raising Section 5 to the "highest priority of the Voting Section of the Civil Rights Division."[7] These events were

1. Reorganization of the Civil Rights Division during 1969, the first year of the Nixon administration
2. Passage of the 1970 Amendments to the Voting Rights Act and defeat of the Nixon proposals for eliminating Section 5
3. The growing strength of civil rights groups in the South
4. Massive redistricting in the South brought on by the 1969 Supreme Court opinion *Allen v. State* and by results of the 1970 census.
5. Pressure for submission guidelines from conservative white leaders in the South

The Nixon Reorganization. In October 1969, the early days of the Nixon administration, a change took place in the organization of the Civil Rights Division. The division was reorganized along functional rather than geographic lines, and as a consequence a reshuffling occurred in CRD. People were given the opportunity to choose their new area of work, then these were submitted to the assistant attorney general's office, out of which new assignments were made. Some employees wanted out of the education area and into voting. Others wanted to continue in voting, and they asked to remain.

Whatever the real reasons for the reorganization—greater political control of the sections or a more effective utilization of legal skills — its effect was to establish a cadre of line attorneys, thirteen in all, who were strongly committed to the enforcement of voting rights laws. These Voting Section lawyers became *the* Section 5 experts and, with the addition of paralegal analysts in the next few years, they initiated a concerted campaign to implement Section 5. In the absence of other events, however, the reorganization alone would not have accounted for the dramatic increase in the number of submissions on voting changes received by DOJ after 1970.

Congressional Extension of the Act. Congressional debates in 1969 and 1970 on the question of extending the Voting Rights Act indicated that Attorney General John Mitchell seriously questioned the workability of Section 5. During the summer of 1969 he appeared before the House Judiciary Committee to argue against the extension of the act in its original shape and scope. Not prepared to support "regional legislation" and opposed to an outright extension of the act as well as to its enforcement, Mitchell suggested that (1) preclearance procedures under Section 5 be abandoned as unnecessary and (2) the act be amended to require CRD's Voting Section to monitor voting changes nationally; if discriminatory voting changes were discovered, Mitchell proposed, the DOJ should go to district court and seek the traditional relief. "In contrast to the 1965 Act, our proposal leaves the decisions to the court where in our opinion it belongs; it properly places the burden of proof *on the government* and not on the states, . . . it is not necessary any more to discriminate against these southern states."[8]

Furthermore, Mitchell's position with respect to voting changes did not include either redistricting or annexation plans. There was an instant response to administration thinking. Representative William McCullough, ranking Republican member of the House Judiciary Committee, was so outraged by Mitchell's suggestions that he countered, "the proposal sweeps broadly into those areas where the need is least, and retreats from those areas where the need is the greatest. The administration has created a remedy for which there is no wrong and leaves grievous wrongs without adequate remedy."

In the ensuing months, the Nixon administration, having alienated the civil rights forces with these potential modifications, proceeded to alienate the southern forces by not supporting the proposals in Congress. Finally, Congress passed the 1970 amendments to the 1965 VRA. The legislation extended the act for an additional five-year period, ended the use of literacy tests nationally, lowered the voting age in federal elections, and standardized residency requirements. Congressional insistence on retaining the preclearance procedures signaled a strong mandate to the CRD to improve the enforcement of Section 5.

Growing strength of rights groups. Still another element in the unfolding 1969–1971 Section 5 enforcement scenario was the growing strength of civil rights organizations in the Deep South. David Norman, a former DOJ official in the Nixon administration, has commented that a growing force pushing VRA enforcement came from the civil rights groups as they became adept at using Section 5.

Recognition of the section's importance and the subsequent reporting of violations by civil rights groups had the effect of putting additional pressure on the CRD just as they were gearing up for intensive work with Section 5. One reason for CRD and Voting Section hesitancy was uncertainty over the scope and dimensions of Section 5. Attorney General Mitchell had excluded annexation and redistricting from coverage; he also suggested that the burden of proof fall upon the government with respect to demonstrating discrimination. The staff attorneys in the Voting Section believed that Section 5 covered annexation and redistricting, but they were constrained by the policymakers in DOJ. This impasse was cleared up in 1969 when the Supreme Court announced *Allen v. State.*

Allen v. State Board of Elections. In 1969 the Supreme Court, in *South Carolina v. Katzenbach,* validated Section 5 as constitutional. While admitting that the VRA was an "uncommon exercise of congressional power," Chief Justice Earl Warren (reviewing the history of racial turbulence in the South) concluded that "exceptional conditions can justify legislative measures not otherwise appropriate."[9] The test used to measure the constitutionality of Section 5 was the one Chief Justice Marshall had used in 1819: "Let the end be legitimate,. . . then all means. . . consistent with the letter and spirit of the Constitution are constitutional." Three years later, in *Allen v. State Board of Elections*, which combined three Mississippi cases with a Virginia case, the Supreme Court defined the scope of Section 5.

The Supreme Court concluded that "the Voting Rights Act was aimed at the subtle, as well as the obvious, state regulations which have the effect of denying citizens their right to vote because of their race."[10] The Court stated that Section 5 ought to be literally construed and that lower courts would not be able to restrict the limit of the Section 5 protection.

In *Allen* the Court also addressed the issue of preclearance submission procedures. Appellees had contended that since no formal preclearance submissions were required by the attorney general, their Section 5 obligations were fulfilled whenever the attorney general became aware of state enactments. After taking notice of the absence of formal procedures, the Court stated that the Voting Rights Act "required that the State in some unambiguous and recordable manner submit any legislation or regulation. . . directly to the Attorney General with a request for his consideration. . . ."

Development of Submission Regulations. As these events—political, legal, and administrative—increased the pressure on the covered jurisdictions to submit proposed voting changes for review, the local units and their representatives in Congress began to insist on some firm guidelines from DOJ. The strongest demand for regulations came from conservative southern lawyers who had to comply with the act but were in need of detailed instructions. Complaints were made "at the highest level in the Nixon Administration" about the lack of specific directions. In response, the CRD prepared and circulated drafts of proposed regulations to these officials and to civil rights groups for their comments and suggestions. The regulations, known as 28 CFR Part 51, were published in September 1971.

From 1965 to 1969, the DOJ received 323 voting changes for preclearance. Since the events of 1969–1971, more than thirty thousand submissions have been received by the Voting Section of CRD. As constructed, the rules enabled the covered jurisdictions to file preclearance papers with either the U.S. District Court for the District of Columbia or with the attorney general. A state thus could opt for either administrative or judicial routes in its attempt to legitimatize a proposed voting change. Filing with the Justice Department, however, enables the states and local subdivisions covered by the Voting Rights Acts to obtain a more rapid determination (withing sixty days) of the acceptability of proposed changes in election laws. For this reason virtually all of the local actions since 1971 regulations were published have been directed to the Department of Justice rather than to the U.S. district court. Enforcement of the act therefore has become the primary responsibility of administrative officials in the Department of Justice — particularly of the staff lawyers of the Civil Rights Division, Voting Section. These individuals have represented the national government in the struggle for voting rights in the federal system. To the administrator in the Department of Justice has fallen the burdensome task of examining voting changes submitted by the states and subdivisions covered under the 1965 voting rights legislation.

ADMINISTRATIVE PROCESSING OF PRECLEARANCE SUBMISSIONS.

In 1980, local jurisdictions submitted almost five thousand voting "changes" to the Department of Justice.[11] While a single letter from a submitting authority often contains multiple changes, such as moving six polling places or sixty-seven annexations, nevertheless each individual change has to be researched and analyzed. Primary responsibility for processing the daily load of approximately twenty changes rests with the attorneys and the paralegal staff of the Civil Rights Division's Voting Section. The Voting Section is divided for operational purposes into the submission unit and the litigative staff, as illustrated by Table 11.1.

Before the 1975 amendments, submission unit attorneys reviewed voting changes with assistance from five paraprofessionals who were paired with attorneys to serve as "law clerks." With the anticipated growth in submissions resulting from new minority language provisions, six more paraprofessionals were added as part of a February 1976 reorganization. After a period of intensive training by Voting Section attorneys, the research analysts (their preferred title) assumed principal responsibility for examination of voting changes.

Table 11.1. Voting section professional and paraprofessional staffing as of July 1977

Chief		
Deputy chief[a]		
Submission unit		*Litigative staff*
1 senior attorney advisor[b]	1	assistant for litigation
1 paraprofessional director	13	attorneys
11 paraprofessionals	2	paraprofessionals

[a]Responsible for administration of the voting section and election coverage activity.
[b]Also performs litigative activity.

The Section 5 submission unit's paraprofessionals and their director come from a diverse background. Some are law students for a time; others are simply college graduates who qualified for this GS 5–10 level job; and others have been clerical employees in DOJ. Hired through standard Civil Service procedures, no special analytic skills are required. (The exceptions are the few paraprofessionals hired for their bilingual skills.) In commenting on the prime talent he looks for in a candidate, David Hunter, the attorney responsible for the submissions unit, stated, "Just the ability to speak to people in Mississippi or Alabama or Georgia, blacks and whites. Just an intelligent person who can learn just what we are looking for. Just willing to deal with people a bit resourcefully.... Writing ability is very important because they have a lot of letters to write." No explicit training manual for the analysts exists; instead, the training is essentially an on-the-job learning process.

Because the 1965 legislation insists that submissions be acted upon within a sixty-day time limit, these thirteen DOJ staffers function under conditions unique among federal programs. That is, *they cannot delay*. Failure to review a submission in sixty days results in its preclearance, even if the proposed change is discriminatory. Given the volume of changes and the shortage of personnel the mechanics of preclearance unsurprisingly involve a series of routinized tasks and discretionary judgments. Table 11.2 illustrates the process.[12]

Designed to satisfy the recordkeeping requirements of Section 51.26 of the 1965 act, the initial preclearance phase simply creates the documentation necessary for subsequent decisions. In contrast, the second phase of the preclearance process is pivotal because the paralegal research analysts make the initial (and normally upheld) determinations with respect to whether or not the proposed change has a discriminatory purpose or effect. Their casework includes not only gathering and analyzing sufficient information about the submission, but also making the critical decision on action to be followed by the Voting Section.

Phase two of the process appears to be a rather ordinary and straightforward approach to processing submissions. Underlying these standard operating procedures, however, are three points of decision that entail substantial discretion. First, the preparation and analysis of the demographic and legal information about each change is in the hands of paraprofessionals who possess neither demographic/statistical skills nor legal training. Since Section 51.10 mandates that the covered jurisdictions transmit all relevant materials, including census data, there is room for differences of opinion about the quality of submitted data, as well as the distinct possibility of data manipulation. In most cases, this issue does not pose a serious problem. In some of the more extreme situations, however, the absence of analytic abilities within the submission unit has led to underestimation of the minority population.

The second major point of administrative discretion develops out of the standard procedure "to telephone minority persons in the locality to see if the voting change is going to bother them." A contact file of minority elected officials, minority group leaders, and other interested and informed individuals is maintained by the Voting Section for use by the attorneys and research analysts. The number of local minority contacts made per case depends, as one paraprofessional

Table 11.2.　Voting change preclearance process

Phase one: initial processing

1. Letter from submitting authority passes through DOJ mail sort and arrives at Section 5 office

Day 1
(60-day
time
limit
begins
here)

2. Paraprofessional staff member logs submission in triplicate on an information card which serves as
   a. a label for the submission file to be maintained
   b. input data for computer listings
   c. a control card for compliance followup

3. To complete the information card, the paraprofessional
   a. notes type of change(s) in the submission
   b. assigns each change in the submission an identification number (change number)
   c. dates receipt of submission by Section 5 office
   d. estimates review completion date
   e. describes submitting jurisdiction
   f. lists name of the paraprofessional assigned to analyze the submission

4. Paraprofessional director reads letter from submitting authority and assigns the submission to a paraprofessional, giving consideration to the geographical origin and complexity of the change and to the experience of the paraprofessional

5. Some letters received by the Section 5 office are not submissions, but rather requests for information; these receive appropriate responses from the paraprofessional director at this point

Phase two: case analysis by paraprofessional

1. Previous record is checked for information, for example:
   a. name(s) of city attorney
   b. form of government
   c. population characteristics

2. If no previous file exists, new record is developed

3. Demographic and legal information about the proposed voting change obtained, for example:
   a. nature of the area annexed
   b. location and number of new polling places
   c. existence of petitions to annex

4. Contacts made with minorities in the affected area and officials of the submitting authority

5. On the basis of this research, the paraprofessional recommends one of the following courses of action:
   a. the submission cannot be reviewed under Section 5 at the time
   b. additional information should be requested from the submitting authority
   c. no objection should be interposed
   d. an objection should be interposed

Phase three: final decision

Day 45

1. Paraprofessional director makes a procedural review of the case analysis

Days 45   2. Legal review and decision made by senior attorney, Section 5 office
to 60

     3. If decision is either "no objection" or "change cannot be reviewed under Section 5 at the time," then a standard letter is returned to the submitting authority
End of preclearance process

     4. If decision is to "object," then
       a. Section 5 attorney prepares letter of objection
       b. Chief, Voting Section, reviews letter of objection
       c. Deputy Assistant Attorney General, Civil Rights Division, reviews letter of objection
       d. Assistant Attorney General, Civil Rights Division, reviews and signs letter of objection
Day 60   e. Letter of objection mailed to submitting authority
End of preclearance process
Litigation staff involved

Phase four: followup on request for additional information

     1. If submitting authority complies, then preclearance begins again at Day 1

Day 90   2. If thirty days elapse without receipt of additional information, Section 5 office initiates a memo requesting an FBI investigation

     3. Memo reviewed by Chief, Observer Program

     4. FBI visits submitting authority

     5. Usually, submitting authority mails requested information
Preclearance process begins
again at Day 1

put it, "on the type of change—the more significant the change, the more contacts required." To supplement the documents from the submitting authority, contacts with local white officials normally are made. From this brief description it becomes obvious that the procedures used by the paraprofessionals place them in an adjudicatory rule.

This judgment takes tangible form in the recommendation on the case. While the paraprofessional can choose one of four options, it is the decision to object or not to object that is crucial to all parties. This choice, although ostensibly based on detailed information, confronts a fundamental substantive problem in the preclearance process: under what circumstances and given what characteristics will a voting change be objected to by the Department of Justice? Put another way, what is the "operational definition" of discriminatory purpose or effect as discussed in Section 5?[13]

In essence, the determination of discrimination has became routinized through the adoption of some elementary rules. The research analysts are trained to spot "red flags" or "suspicious-type changes." These include at-large elections, reductions in the number of polling places, changes in the location of polling places, and redistricting. Proposed changes such as these alert the paralegals to investigate the motive behind the change and the potential impact of the change.

Investigating motivation and impact in often isolated localities throughout the South and Southwest without a field staff puts a premium on the telephone calls to on-site contacts. Even after a number of contacts and extensive documentation, however, the operationalization of discrimination ultimately becomes "situational." In the words of the paraprofessional director, Janet Blizzard, "One looks at the circumstances of the change: the area, the people affected, what's going to hurt the people."

The final phase within the sixty-day time limit is the most hectic, with letters usually being mailed at the last possible moment. Casework on a proposed change must reach the paraprofessional director's desk no later than day forty-five for procedural review. Legal review and final recommendation by the submission unit attorney is the last step. Describing this process, the current submission unit staff attorney, David Hunter, has said:

> I want them [paraprofessionals] to do all the research on it and let the decision be made a higher level than it is actually done. If they recommend objection and we are not objecting, we can just change it. If they recommend a no objection, and haven't done the homework on it, it's likely to go out that way....I might not catch it, or it just might be visible to me while I'm checking. It's better that they made mistakes, instead of doing too much.

This is "discretionary justice" in its classic form. Because the review and signature steps in regard to interposing an objection will catch almost all errors, the chance of mistake is more likely in the finding of "no objection."

When the decision is to seek additional information from the submitting authority, a subsequent procedure is followed. If the local officials respond promptly, they merely go back to day one and begin preclearance over again. However, if they delay more than thirty days, the Section 5 office initiates a memo that sends the FBI to the community. The almost automatic nature of phase four comes out in this description by the Voting Section chief, Gerald Jones:

> If they are out thirty days or more, we will send the FBI out to meet with the official and find out what the problem is. Usually that has the best result, when the FBI goes out and visits. We are getting a lot more of the submissions completed now than we once did.

Use of the FBI in this fashion is seen as a free resource by the Voting Section in that it serves as part of the section's surrogate field staff. Though Voting Section personnel believe that use of the Bureau "is fairly effective in stimulating a response," a 1978 General Accounting Office report on voting rights enforcement suggests that local officials do not necessarily tremble and quiver before the federal "muscle." Some jurisdictions have not responded in over two years after receipt of a request for additional information about a proposed voting change.[14] Even more damaging, the proposed changes are often implemented and elections are conducted without completion of the preclearance process.

CONSEQUENCES OF DISCRETIONARY JUSTICE

What becomes clear from the previous discussion is that in operationalizing "discriminatory purpose and effect," DOJ officials have evolved some elementary decision rules that they call upon when confronted with a new submission. However, these are essentially cognitive rules that individual research analysts have come to learn from experience, rather than any formal set of guidelines for identifying suspicious or potentially objectionable changes. Two important consequences flow from this situation: (1) covered jurisdictions are at least partially in the dark as to what counts as evidence of nondiscrimination; and (2) in the absence of rules that set down general principles governing the acceptability of certain types of voting changes, decisions regarding the acceptability of submitted changes are frequently negotiated.

The Department of Justice has made some effort to inform covered jurisdictions about the requirements of Section 5. After the Civil Rights Division published the guidelines known as 28 CFR 51, Voting Section attorneys traveled to some jurisdictions to meet with local officials. By 1973 information packets (containing the amended 1965 act, the 1971 regulations, and a request to send all preclearances to either DOJ or to the district court for a declaratory judgment) were sent to all covered jurisdictions.

However, since the burden of proof under Section 5 is on the submitting authority, it is important for covered jurisdictions to know precisely what counts as evidence of nondiscrimination. Regulation 28 CFR 51 informs them about the requirement to submit voting changes for preclearance; it tells them about the kinds of changes that must be submitted and about the types of supporting evidence required; but it does not provide much information about the criteria DOJ officials will apply in deciding whether or not to enter an objection.[15]

Attorneys in the Voting Section of CRD believe that over 90 percent of all voting changes are reported to the attorney general, and that those that remain unreported are probably the least dangerous types of change with respect to diluting the black vote. Of those reported, approximately 95 percent are precleared. A major factor in the high preclearance rate is the process of informal discussion—advisement, assistance, and negotiation—between local officials and DOJ officials. The Voting Section apparently does not want to dramatically interfere in local policymaking processes and prefers to work cooperatively with local officials in the covered jurisdictions. This posture is illustrated by David Hunter, the attorney in charge of preclearance submissions:

> [Local jurisdictions] want guidelines; they want to know what we are going to look for. They're going to revise their city charter and the city attorney will call me up to ask...and this is a widespread type of request....They have a job to do and they want to get our clearance....we'll do what we can for them....we try to make things go smoothly for them so they can hold elections.

There can be little doubt that the strategy of negotiating over the difficult parts of potentially objectionable preclearance submissions has facilitated the task of obtaining compliance with Section 5 of the Voting Rights Act. That is a very positive accomplishment. However, this strategy, no matter what its virtues, is problematical in two important ways. First, it may produce compliance at marginal levels of acceptability. Negotiated justice can produce "no objection" whenever the affected black population is not harmed by proposed voting changes, although relative black voting strength may not have have been substantially improved. It may permit an unconstitutional scheme to be replaced with a less obnoxious, but possibly still discriminatory, procedure. Second, a negotiation strategy is not very helpful in providing guidance as to what counts as evidence of nondiscrimination. On this count it is deficient as judged by the Davis-Lowi standard. As Lowi has noted, "There is an implicit rule in every bargained or adjudicated case, but it cannot be known to the bargainer until he knows the outcome, and its later application must be deciphered by lawyers representing potential cases."[16] These are significant compliance dilemmas that result from exercising administrative discretion in the manner of negotiated justice.

In summary, negotiated justice is a double-edged sword. This individualized approach to obtaining compliance usually achieves the substantive objectives of the Voting Rights Act. However, negotiated justice transpires in the absence of specified decision criteria well known in advance to those who are obligated to comply with Section 5. For DOJ decision makers, the problem is less severe because the experience of past decisions provides guides, or rules of thumb, for their future decisions. However, local jurisdictions, which are much less frequently involved and are not themselves parties to past decisions involving other jurisdictions, are not much better off in terms of knowing "what counts" as the result of the negotiated justice process.

It is doubtful that DOJ officials could ever formulate a complete set of criteria setting down exactly what counts as evidence of nondiscrimination—the nature of the subject mitigates against very precise rules. Perhaps, however, they can do better than they are doing. If local jurisdictions are required to comply with federal regulations, they are entitled to guidance as to the criteria by which their preclearance submissions will be judged. (Hypothetical cases drawn up with real situations in mind are a possible alternative to rules enunciating general principles.)

The essence of the principle of rule of law in a democratic society is that it provides a basis for ensuring the accountability of official actions. Maintaining the delicate balance between substantive justice (guaranteeing an acceptable degree of minority voting rights) through negotiation and procedural justice (informing local jurisdictions of the standards by which they will be judged) is a difficult task. Department of Justice administrators should be constantly mindful of this problem.

NOTES

1. DISCRETION FITS DEMOCRACY: AN ADVOCATE'S ARGUMENT

1. See Chapter 2 for discussion of the law implementation system. The law system is viewed herein as a subcategory of the general political system.

2. Kenneth Culp Davis, *Discretionary Justice: A Preliminary Overview* (Baton Rouge: Louisiana Univ. Press, 1969), 221.

3. Ronald Dworkin, *Taking Rights Seriously* (Cambridge, Mass.: Harvard Univ. Press, 1977), 31.

4. For an enlightening discussion of this point, see Gordon S. Wood, *The Creation of the American Republic, 1776–1787* (Chapel Hill: Univ. of North Carolina Press, 1969), and the *Federalist Papers* (New York: Mentor Books, 1962), especially Numbers 10, 48, and 51.

5. For a discussion of the role of symbols, see Murray Edelman, *The Symbolic Uses of Politics* (Urbana: Univ. Illinois Press, 1964).

6. See the recent work by Howard Ball, Dale Krane, and Thomas Lauth, *Comprised Compliance: Implementation of the 1965 Voting Rights Act* (Westport, Conn.: Greenwood Press, 1982) for a discussion of this sort of political behavior.

7. For a stimulating discussion of this point, see William M. Sullivan, *Reconstructing Public Philosophy* (Berkeley: Univ. of California Press, 1982).

8. Brian Berry, *The Liberal Theory of Justice* (Oxford: Clarendon Press, 1973), 166.

9. Possibly the most influential single source articulating the dominance of Lockean notions has been Louis Hartz, *The Liberal Tradition in America* (New York: Harcourt, Brace, Janovich, 1955); a good piece that critically investigates the Hartz thesis is Mark E. Kann, "Challenging Lockean Liberalism in America: The Case of Debs and Hilquit," *Political Theory* 8, no. 2(May 1980):203–22.

10. For a discussion of the nonpolitical intentions of liberal thinking, see Sheldon Wolin, *Politics and Vision* (Boston: Little, Brown, 1960), Chaps. 9 and 10.

11. According to Giovanni Sartori equality is a "protest ideal." See Giovianni Sartori, *Democratic Theory* (New York: Frederick A. Praeger, 1965), 227.

12. Dworkin, *Taking Rights Seriously,* 227.

13. S. I. Benn and R. S. Peters, *The Principles of Political Thought: Social Foundations of the Democratic State* (New York: Free Press, 1959), 126.

14. John Rawls, *A Theory of Justice* (Cambridge, Mass.: Harvard Univ., Belknap Press, 1971), 75.

15. For a succinct discussion of democratic procedures, see Robert A. Dahl, *Dilemmas of Pluralist Democracy: Autonomy v. Control* (New Haven: Yale Univ. Press, 1982), 6.

16. For other liberal thinkers, see E. K. Bramsted and K. J. Melhuish, eds., *Western Liberalism: A History in Documents from Locke to Croce* (New York: Longman, 1978), 589–98.

17. Kenneth Culp Davis, *Discretionary Justice;* Theodore J. Lowi, *The End of Liberal-*

ism (New York: W. W. Norton, 1969). For a response to the "realist" persuasion see Lane David, "The Cost of Realism: Contemporary Restatements of Democracy," *Western Political Quarterly* 17(Mar. 1964):37–46; for a response concerning those who would limit potentials see Joseph H. Carens, *Equality, Moral Incentives, and the Market* (Chicago: Univ. of Chicago Press, 1981).

18. George C. Edwards III and Ira Sharkansky, *The Policy Predicament: Making and Implementing Public Policy* (San Francisco: W. H. Freeman, 1978), 235.

2. THE POLITICS OF DISCRETIONARY JUSTICE AMONG CRIMINAL JUSTICE AGENCIES

1. Discretion was documented by the National Commission on Law Observance and Enforcement (the Wickersham Commission) in 1931 and found thriving upon revisitation by the President's Commission on Law Enforcement and Administration of Justice in 1967; *Brady v. U.S.,* 397 U.S. 742 (1970), and *North Carolina v. Alford,* 400 U.S. 25 (1970).

2. Richard Quinney, ed., *Criminal Justice in America: A Critical Understanding* (Boston: Little, Brown, 1974), 236.

3. Douglas Greenberg, *Crime and Law Enforcement in the Colony of New York, 1691–1776* (Ithaca: Cornell Univ. Press, 1976), 99, 190.

4. Samuel Walker, *Popular Justice: A History of American Criminal Justice* (New York: Oxford Univ. Press, 1980), 25–26.

5. Walker, *Popular Justice,* 219.

6. Marvin Frankel, *Criminal Sentences: Law Without Order* (New York: Hill and Wang, 1972); George F. Cole, *The American System of Criminal Justice* (North Scituate, Mass.: Duxbury Press, 1979), 23; David W. Neubauer, *America's Courts and the Criminal Justice System* (North Scituate, Mass.: Duxbury, 1979), 21; and Alan Kalmanoff, *Criminal Justice: Enforcement and Administration* (Boston: Little, Brown, 1976).

7. Walker, *Popular Justice,* 7.

8. Lewis R. Katz, *The Justice Imperative* (Cincinnati: Anderson, 1980), 21–22.

9. William C. Louthan, "Relationships Among Police, Court, and Correctional Agencies," *Policy Studies Journal* 3(Autumn 1974):30.

10. Cole, *American System,* 63–64.

11. W. Boyd Littrell, *Bureaucratic Justice* (Beverly Hills: Sage, 1979).

12. Walker, *Popular Justice,* 6.

13. Quinney, *Criminal Justice in America,* 192.

14. Neubauer, *America's Courts,* 107–108.

15. Herbert M. Kritzer, "Court Reform Through Role Reform: The Role of the Judge as an Instrument of Reform," paper presented at the Midwest Political Science Association Meetings, Cincinnati, April 15–18, 1981.

16. Cole, *American System,* 23–24, 170–71, 261–62.

17. Malcolm M. Feeley, *The Process is the Punishment: Handling Cases in Lower Criminal Court* (New York: Russell Sage, 1979).

18. Suzann R. Thomas Buckle and Leonard G. Buckle, *Bargaining for Justice: Case Disposition and Reform in the Criminal Courts* (New York: Praeger, 1977), 64–65.

19. Neubauer, *America's Courts,* 414–15.

20. Kalmanoff, *Criminal Justice: Enforcement and Administration,* 225–31.

3. THE POLITICS OF POLICE DISCRETION

1. Wayne Francis, *Legislative Issues in the Fifty States* (Chicago: Rand McNally, 1967), 77, indicates governors have considerable influence on the way policies are made in the states, but law enforcement apparently is not a high priority.

2. According to Herman Goldstein, *Policing a Free Society* (Cambridge, Mass.: Ballinger, 1977) state governments played a minimal role affecting local policing until passage of the Omnibus Crime Control Act of 1968.

3. This is based on the assumption that police discretion issues continue to be relatively minor concerns of interest groups who could motivate action, and a concern that does not have significant political appeal for state governors to warrant their involvement in the issue.

4. Kenneth C. Davis, *Police Discretion* (St. Paul, Minn.: West, 1975), 81.

5. Wayne LaFave, *Modern Criminal Law* (St. Paul, Minn.: West, 1978), 41.

6. Full enforcement legislation in Ohio, Michigan, California, Indiana, and Nebraska exemplifies cases in which the legislation was enacted primarily to establish city and county governments rather than to explicitly define the duties of law enforcement officers, particularly with regard to arrest decisions. Ohio *Laws*, c. 96; Mich. *Acts* (1895), no. 215, c. 12, sec. 4; Calif. *Statutes* (1883), c. 75, sec. 93; Ind. *Acts* (1905), c. 129, sec. 161; Nebr. *Laws* (1901), c. 18, sec. 30.

7. Arizona, Arkansas, Colorado, Connecticut, Delaware, Georgia, Idaho, Illinois, Indiana, Iowa, Kansas, Kentucky, Massachusetts, Michigan, Minnesota, Missouri, New Mexico, New York, North Dakota, Ohio, Oklahoma, Oregon, Pennsylvania, and Texas.

8. Herbert Wechsler, "The Challenge of a Modern Penal Code," *Harvard Law Review* 65(1952):112.

9. William A. Platz, "The Criminal Code," *Wisconsin Law Review* (1956):350; Jerold H. Israel, "The Process of Penal Law Reform—A Look at the Proposed Michigan Revised Criminal Code," *Wayne Law Review* 14(1968):772.

10. Ariz. *Rev. Stat. Ann.* §18.65.080 (1969); Ark. *Stat. Ann.* §17-3601(5) (1979); Colo. *Rev. Stat.* §31-4-112 (1973); Conn. *Gen. Stat.* §54-1f (1981); Del. *Code Ann. tit.* 11 §8302 (1974); Idaho *Code* §19-4804, (1979); Ill. *Ann. Stat.* chapt. 125 §82 (Smith-Hurd Supp. 1976); Ind. *Code* §17-3-5-2, 18-1-11-4 (1976); Iowa *Code* §748.4 (1977) (repealed); Ky. *Rev. Stat.* §70.570 (1962) (repealed); Mass. *Ann. Laws* chapt. 41, §98 (Michie/Law Coop. 1973); Mich. *Comp. Laws* §92.4 (1979); (Mich. *Stat. Ann.* §5-1752 (Callaghan 1978); Minn. *Stat.* §387.03 (1980); Mo. *Rev. Stat.* §57.100 (1978); N.Mex. *Stat. Ann.* §§3-132, 4-41-2 (1978, 1980); Ohio *Rev. Code Ann.* §737.11 (Page 1976).

11. For this Iowa work a limited number of interviews were conducted by the author with state legislators, police officials, and other state and local officials knowledgeable about state criminal justice problems. While the scope and extent of such interviews preclude strong empirical verification, it was possible to verify some general conclusions.

12. Four states that substantially completed their revisions prior to 1970 were selected—Illinois (1962), Michigan (1968), Minnesota (1969), and Kentucky (1970), and four states that have taken action since the mid-seventies were selected—Arkansas (1976), Arizona (1977), Iowa (1978), and Missouri (1979).

13. Israel, "Process of Penal Law Reform," 814.

14. Ibid., 814.

15. See "Public Disorder Statutes in Iowa: An Evaluation of Existing Statutes and the Proposed Revision," *Iowa Law Review* 57 (1972): 882–83; Jeffrey Bell, "Legislative Notes: Disorderly Conduct and Loitering—A Modern Approach to Traditional Legislation," *Arkansas Law Review* 30(1976):203–4.

16. Terry R. Kirkpatrick, "Arrest Citation and Summons: The Supreme Court Takes a Giant Step Forward," *Arkansas Law Review* 30(1976):146–48. The citation system was not the direct product of legislative action in Arkansas. In 1971 the Arkansas Criminal Code Revision Commission was given the responsibility of recommending changes in the substantive and procedural criminal law. Recommendations for substantive changes were acted upon by the legislature and recommendations for procedural changes were promulgated by the Arkansas Supreme Court. Action on citations was part of the recommendations by the Code Revision Commission and was carried out by the Arkansas Supreme Court.

17. Ibid., 145.

18. Iowa *Code* (1981), sections 805.6, 805.8.

19. American Law Institute, *Model Case of Pre-Arraignment Procedure* (Philadelphia: American Law Institute, 1973), section 120.2.

20. U.S. Commission on Civil Rights, *Who Is Guarding the Guardians? A Report on Police Practices* (Washington, D.C.: Government Printing Office, 1981), 37.

21. Kansas State Advisory Committee, "Policing in Wichita" (Washington, D.C.: Government Printing Office, 1980), 13-20.

22. American Law Institute, *Model Penal Code* (Philadelphia: American Law Institute, 1962), section 3.07.

23. See Missouri *Advisory Committee Report,* 103-4, and Mo. *Rev. Stat.,* section 563.046.3(2)(a) (1978 cum. supp.).

24. Massachusetts Criminal Law Revision Commission, *Proposed Criminal Code of Massachusetts* (New York: Lawyers Co-operative, 1972), chap. 264; Jack M. Kress, *Prescription for Justice: The Theory and Practice of Sentencing Guidelines* (Cambridge, Mass.: Ballinger, 1980), 3.

25. R. J. Gerber, "Arizona's New Criminal Code: An Overview and Critique," *Arizona State Law Journal* (1977): 502-6.

26. Ariz. *Rev. Stat. Ann.* (1978), section 13-702.

27. *State v. Bly,* 127 Arizona 370, 621 P.2d 279 (1980); *State v. Jenson,* 123 Arizona 72, 597 P.2d 554 (App. 1979).

28. George T. Felkenes, *The Criminal Justice System: Its Functions and Personnel* (Englewood Cliffs, N.J.: Prentice-Hall, 1973), 145-50.

29. "The evolution of the American criminal justice system has separated the responsibilities of the police from the prosecutor and has moved toward clearer divisions of responsibility." Joan Jacoby, *The American Prosecutor: A Search for Identity* (Lexington, Mass.: Lexington Books, D. C. Heath, 1980), 109.

30. Jacoby, *American Prosecutor,* 30: Gregory H. Williams, "Maryland State's Attorneys" (M.A. thesis, University of Maryland, 1969), 65.

31. Ohio Advisory Committee to the U.S. Commission on Civil Rights, *Policing in Cincinnati, Ohio: Official Policy vs. Civilian Reality* (1981), 68-70; Kansas Advisory Committee to the U.S. Commission of Civil Rights, *Police Community Relations in the City of Wichita and Sedgwick County* (1980), 67-68; U.S. Commission on Civil Rights, *Police Practices and the Preservation of Civil Rights* (Washington, D.C.: Government Printing Office, 1978), 2.

32. Raymond B. Fosdick, *American Police Systems* (New York: Century, 1920, reprinted 1969 by Patterson Smith), 58-117, 212-13; see also Frank J. Goodnow, *Municipal Government* (New York: Century, 1925), and Bruce Smith, *Police Systems in the United States* (New York: Harper, 1940).

33. Contemporary Studies Project, "Administrative Control of Police Discretion," *Iowa Law Review* 58(April 1973):913; see also note 31.

34. James R. Hudson, "Police Review Boards and Police Accountability," *Law and Contemporary Problems* 36(1971):521-28.

35. *Hoggard v. City of Richmond,* 172 Va. 145, 200 S.E. 610 (1939); *Britt v. Ocala,* 65 S.2d 753 (1953).

36. Kenneth Culp Davis, *Administrative Law Text* (St. Paul, Minn.: West Publishing, 1972), 466-68.

37. Because of the difficulty of bringing suit and winning against municipalities and their officers at the state level, many citizens turned to the federal courts to remedy improper treatment by local police officials. Police misconduct suits were frequently brought against individual officers under 42 USC 1983, or the so-called Civil Rights Statute, *Monroe v. Pape,* 365 U.S. 167, 191 n. 50 (1961). But, like efforts at the state level, that course of action had inherent drawbacks. Most notably, the case of *Monroe v. Pape* held that a municipality was not a "person" within the meaning of section 1983, and consequently a municipality could not be held liable for acts of its employees which deprived citizens of their constitutional rights. The past few years have seen remarkable evolution of the doctrine enunciated in *Pape.* The U.S. Supreme Court, in an unusual reinterpretation of the legislative history of the Civil Rights Act, found that under some circumstances municipalities should be liable for the action of the employees. The Supreme Court in *Monell v. New York* overruled *Monroe v. Pape* and began to open the door for suits against municipalities for the tortious acts of its employees. *Monell v. New York,* 437 U.S. 658,

700–701 (1978). The theory of municipal liability, however, is limited. Rather than finding municipal liability after a showing of tortious action of a city employee or on the theory of respondent superior, the Court in *Monell* said city liability would be found only if the action of the city employee could reasonably be said to represent official policy or informal governmental custom.

38. The lower courts are wrestling with questions such as the degree of negligence necessary to support a Section 1983 claim against a city, what constitutes an informal governmental custom, and other problems arising under Section 1983. It is clear that municipalities should want to begin to take a much slower look at the operation and function of their local police departments, particularly their arrest practices. *Leite v. City of Providence,* 463 F. Supp 585 (D.C.R.I. 1978); *McNamara v. Moody,* 606 F.2d 621 (5th Cir. 1979); *McClelland v. Facteau,* 610 F.2d 693 (10th Cir. 1979); *Echols v. Strickland,* 28 Criminal Law Reporter 2092 (U.S. Dist. Ct. S. Tex. 1980); *Smith v. Hill,* 510 F.Supp 767 (D.C. Utah 1981). The distinct possibility that claims of violation of constitutionally protected rights of equal protection and due process in the arrest decision can be successful surely opens the door to subsequent liability suits against municipalities.

39. Stephen A. Schiller, "More Light on a Low Visibility Function: The Selective Enforcement of the Laws, Parts 1–4," *Police Law Quarterly* (Spring 1973), 37; see also James Q. Wilson, *Varieties of Police Behavior* (Cambridge: Harvard Univ. Press, 1968), 278–99.

40. Wilson, *Police Behavior,* 294.

41. *Chastain v. Civil Service Board of Orlando,* 327 So.2d 230 (Fla. 4th Dist. Ct. App. 1976); and *City of St. Petersburg v. Reed,* 330 So.2d 256 (Fla. 2d Dist. Ct. App. 1976).

42. Goldstein, *Policing a Free Society,* 122. For au contra view see *Peterson v. City of Long Beach,* 594 P.2d 477 (Calif. 1979).

43. *United States v. Caceres,* 440 U.S. 741, 99 S.Ct. 1465 (1979).

44. Egon Bittner, *The Function of the Police in Modern Society* (Rockville, Md.: National Institute of Mental Health Center for Studies of Crime and Delinquency, 1970), 52–62.

45. Jerry V. Wilson and Geoffrey M. Alprin, "Controlling Police Conduct: Alternatives to the Exclusionary Rule," *Law and Contemporary Problems* 36 (Autumn 1971):493.

4. JUDICIAL DISCRETION IN PRETRIAL RELEASE

1. Research suggests that the impact of the bail decision extends beyond the question of freedom or imprisonment pending trial. Two early studies of the operation of bail systems (Chicago, by Arthur Beeley, and Philadelphia and New York, by Caleb Foote) found a correlation between the bail status of a defendant and both the verdict and sentences handed down by the court. Conviction rates were higher and sentences stiffer for those denied bail than for those granted pretrial release. See Arthur Beeley, *The Bail System in Chicago* (Chicago: Univ. of Chicago Press, 1966), and Caleb Foote, "Compelling Appearance in Court: Administration of Bail in Philadelphia," *University of Pennsylvania Law Review,* 102(June 1954).

2. K. C. Davis, *Discretionary Justice* (Urbana: Univ. Illinois Press, 1969), 4; *Ohio Rules of Criminal Procedure,* Rule 46A, Bail.

3. Daniel Freed and Patricia Wald, *Bail in the United States: 1964* (Washington, D.C.: Government Printing Office, 1964), 49; Paul B. Wice, *Freedom For Sale* (Lexington, Mass.: Lexington Books, 1974), 7.

4. For a thorough treatment of bail problems and the reform movement, see Wayne H. Thomas Jr., *Bail Reform in America* (Berkeley: Univ. of California Press, 1976).

5. Vera Institute of Justice, *Programs in Criminal Justice Reform: Ten Year Report, 1961–1971* (May 1972).

6. Ibid., 31–35. The findings are in fact much more complicated than presented here, as the discussion of the National Bail Study by Thomas indicates. See Thomas, *Bail Reform,*

Chaps. 4–12; Chap. 21 provides an excellent summary of the impact of OR programs.

7. Dennis Hartmann, "Pretrial Release of an Accused in Ohio: A Proposed Revision of Ohio Bail Laws," *University of Cincinnati Law Review* 41 (1972), 433–34.

8. Hartmann, "Pretrial Revision, Ohio Bail Laws," *UCLR* (1972), 434.

9. The data does not include those released at the discretion of the officer either through citations or station house release. It does not include individuals who posted bond for minor misdemeanors or whom the bondsmen bonded out immediately. The population therefore is the last majority of individuals who are charged with serious crimes in Hamilton County, whether they be misdemeanors or felonies. Although limited thusly, this is the population for whom bail is set by local trial court judges.

5. THE PROSECUTOR'S DISCRETION: OUT OF THE CLOSET, NOT OUT OF CONTROL

1. Norman Abrams, "Internal Policy: Guiding the Exercise of Prosecutorial Discretion," *UCLA Law Review* 19(1971):1,3.

2. Kenneth Culp Davis, *Discretionary Justice in Europe and America* (Urbana: Univ. of Illinois Press, 1976), 70.

3. James Vorenberg, "Narrowing the Discretion of Criminal Justice Officials," *Duke Law Journal* (1976):651, 694.

4. For example, in *Bordenkircher v. Hayes,* 434 U.S. 357 (1978), a state prosecutor carried out a threat made during plea negotiations to reindict the accused on more serious charges, for which he was subject to prosecution, if he did not plead guilty to the original offense. The U.S. Supreme Court upheld the prosecutor's actions in the face of a due process challenge.

5. Thurman Arnold, *The Symbols of Government* (New York: Harcourt, Brace and World, 1935), 160.

6. In Oregon the 1980 cost of new prison building was estimated at $60,000 per cell. This figure is expected to rise to $160,000 per cell by 1985.

7. Gunther Arzt, "Responses to the Growth of Crime in the United States and West Germany: A Comparison of Changes in Criminal Law and Societal Attitudes," *Cornell International Law Journal* 12(1979):43, 49.

8. Arzt, "Responses to Growth," 15. Arzt reports that the crime rate rose in Germany from 1,678,840 reported crimes in 1963 to 3,063,271 in 1976; the total number of sentences increased during that period from 309,268 to 388,767, but the total prison population declined from 43,453 to 35,085.

9. Figures compiled by Eugene Doleschal, National Council on Crime and Delinquency. The ranking is accurate as of Feb. 9, 1982 (telephone conversation).

10. Richard S. Frase, "The Decision to File Federal Criminal Charges: A Quantitative Study of Prosecutorial Discretion," *University of Chicago Law Review* 47(1980):283–84.

11. Sarah J. Cox, "Prosecutorial Discretion: An Overview," *American Criminal Law Review* 13(1976):414–15.

12. In 1980 the U.S. Supreme Court upheld a Texas habitual offender statute in the case of *Rummel v. Estelle,* 445 U.S. 375. Rummel was charged with obtaining $120.75 by false pretenses, a felony under Texas law. Because he had two prior felony convictions—fraudulent use of a credit card to obtain $80.00 worth of goods and services, and passing a forged check in the amount of $28.36—the prosecution chose to proceed against Rummel under the Texas recidivist statute, which provided: "Whoever shall have been three times convicted of a felony less than capital shall on such third conviction be imprisoned for life in the penitentiary." Rummel's life sentence for offenses totalling $229.11 was found not to be a violation of the Eighth Amendment proscription against cruel and unusual punishment.

13. Leonard R. Mellon, Joan E. Jacoby, and Marion A. Brewer, "The Prosecutor Constrained by His Environment: A New Look at Discretionary Justice in the United States," *Journal of Criminal Law and Criminology* 72(1981):52.

14. Mellon, Jacoby, and Brewer, "The Prosecutor Constrained," 64.

15. Kenneth Culp Davis, *Discretionary Justice: A Preliminary Inquiry* (Baton Rouge: Louisiana State Univ. Press, 1969), 216.

16. Daniel J. Givelber, "The Application of Equal Protection Principles to Selective Enforcement of the Criminal Law," *Univ. Illinois Law Forum* 88(1973):96–100.

17. Arzt, "Responses to Growth," 49–53.

18. Vorenberg, "Narrowing Discretion," at 652.

19. Davis, *Discretionary Justice: A Preliminary Inquiry"* 19; see also Roscoe Pound, "Discretion, Dispensation and Mitigation: The Problem of the Individual Special Case," *New York Univ. Law Review* 35(1960):925, 928–29.

20. Frank W. Miller, *Prosecution: The Decision to Charge a Suspect with a Crime* (Boston: Little, Brown, 1969), 6.

21. System uniformity is discussed at length in Abrams, "Internal Policy," 5–6. Abrams analyzes both vertical and horizontal consistency: vertical decisions are those made by the same or successive prosecutors over time; horizontal decisions are those made by multiple decision makers operating at the same time.

22. For example, the legislature can appropriate funds for full enforcement of any or all laws and by doing so could eliminate much selective enforcement. The legislature can mandate compulsory prosecution, or can attempt to draft laws with such specificity that the avenues for the exercise of discretion are reduced. The legislature can also revise the criminal code to eliminate overcriminalization and antiquated law.

23. *Yick Wo v. Hopkins*, 118 U S 356 (1880), 373–74.

24. Cal 3d 305, 124 Cal Reptr 216 P.2d 56.

25. Roger G. Cramton, "A Comment on Trial-Type Hearings in Nuclear Power Plant Siting," *Virginia Law Review* 58(1972):585, 590.

26. Abrams, "Internal Policy," 51–52.

27. Vorenberg, "Narrowing Discretion," 655.

28. Ibid., 662.

6. DISCRETION AND JUDICIAL SENTENCING

1. Some examples of the neoconservative arguments are Nathan Glazer, "Towards an Imperical Judiciary?" in *The American Commonwealth—1976*, ed. Nathan Glazer and Irving Kristol (New York: Basic Books, 1976), 104–23; Wallace Mendelson, "Mr. Justice Douglas and Government By the Judiciary," *Journal of Politics* 38, no 4(Nov. 1976):918–37.

2. Sheldon Goldman, "In Defense of Justices: Some Thoughts on Reading Professor Mendelson's Mr. Justice Douglas and Goverment by the Judiciary," *Journal of Politics* 38, no. 1(Feb. 1977):152; see also William C. Louthan, *Politics of Justice* (Port Washington, N.Y.: Kennikat, 1979).

3. See H. Frank Way, *Criminal Justice and the American Constitution* (North Scituate, Mass.: Duxbury, 1980).

4. William C. Louthan, *The Politics of Managerial Morality* (Washington, D.C.: Univ. Press of America, 1981), 73–75.

5. Ronald Dworkin, *Taking Rights Seriously* (Cambridge, Mass.: Harvard Univ. Press, 1977), 31.

6. Herbert Jacobs, "Politics and Criminal Prosecution in New Orleans," in *Criminal Justice: Law and Politics*, ed. George F. Cole (North Scituate, Mass.: Duxbury Press, 1972), 149–69.

7. For a fascinating and important recent discussion, see Arthur Selwyn Miller, *Toward Increased Judicial Activism: The Political Role of the Supreme Court* (Westport, Conn.: Greenwood Press, 1982).

8. Kenneth Culp Davis, *Discretionary Justice: A Preliminary Inquiry* (Baton Rouge: Louisiana State Univ. Press, 1969), 133.

9. For a discussion of the centrality of impartiality to justice, see S. I. Benn and R. S. Peters, *The Principles of Political Thought* (New York: Free Press, 1959), Chap. 2.

7. DISCRETION IN THE SENTENCING AND PAROLE PROCESS

1. David Fogel, *We Are the Living Proof: The Justice Model for Corrections* (Cincinnati: W. H. Anderson, 1975), 73; A. Von Hirsch, *Doing Justice: The Choice of Punishment* (New York: Hill & Wang, 1976), 75; A. Von Hirsch and K. J. Hanrahan, *Abolish Parole?* (Washington, D.C.: Law Enforcement Assistance Administration, National Institute of Law Enforcement and Criminal Justice, 1978), 78.

2. Richard McCleary, "How Structural Variables Constrain the Parole Officer's Use of Discretionary Powers," *Social Problems* 23(1975):209-25.

3. A. P. Hier, "Curbing Abuse in the Decision to Grant or Deny Parole," *Harvard Civil Rights Civil Liberties Law Review* 8(1973):419-68.

4. R. C. Pruss, J. R. Stratton, "Parole Revocation Decision-Making: Private Typings and Official Designations," *Federal Probation* 40(1976):76.

5. J. D. Holland, "Parole Release: Federal Circuits Conflict on Applicability of Due Process and Administrative Procedure Act to Parole Release Decision," *Vanderbilt Law Review* 27, 6(1974):1257-77.

6. Tom Burns, G. M. Stalker, *The Management of Innovation* (London: London Taniscotch Press, 1961), 61.

7. C. I. Bernard, *The Functions of the Executive* (Cambridge: Harvard Univ. Press, 1938), 38; C. Argyris, *Personality and Organization* (New York: Harper, 1957), 57.

8. C. I. Bernard, *The Functions of the Executive,* 38; P. N. Blau, *The Dynamics of Bureaucracy* (Chicago: The Univ. of Chicago Press, 1955), 55; C. Perrow, "The Analysis of Goals in Complex Organizations," *American Sociological Review* 26(1961):61.

9. J. D. Thompson and W. J. McEwen, "Organizational Goals and Environment," *American Sociological Review* 23(1958):58.

10. Anthony Downs, *Inside Bureaucracy* (Boston: Little, Brown, 1967), 67.

11. Egon Bittner, *The Function of the Police in Modern Society* (Rockville, Md.: National Institute of Mental Health Center for Studies of Crime and Delinquency, 1970).

12. Robert Carter and Leslie J. Wilkins, "Some Factors in Sentencing Policy," *Journal of Criminal Law, Criminology of Police Science,* 58(1967):67.

13. Amital Etzioni, *A Comparative Analysis of Complex Organizations* (New York: Free Press, 1975), 75.

8. JUDICIAL OVERSIGHT OF DISCRETION IN THE PRISON SYSTEM

I express my appreciation to Professor Barbara A. Schwartz, University of Iowa College of Law, Iowa City, for furnishing background material and providing assistance in the preparation of this article. I also express my appreciation to Theresa O'Connell, Philip Ostien, and Richard Klausner, who, as student legal interns at the University of Iowa, drafted and prepared pleadings and briefs in the Edward Clark case. These pleadings and briefs were invaluable research sources.

1. *Ruffin v. Commonwealth,* 62 Va. (21 Gratt.) 790, 796 (1871).

2. *Siegal v. Razen,* 88 F. Supp. 996, 999 (N.D. Ill. 1949), aff'd. 180 F.2d 785 (7th Cir. 1950), cert. den. 339 U.S. 990 (1950), rehearing den. 340 U.S. 847 (1950).

3. *Coffin v. Reichard,* 143 F.2d 443, 445 (6th Cir. 1944).

4. *Price v. Johnston,* 334 U.S. 266, 285 (1948).

5. *Wolff v. McDonnell,* 418 U.S. 539 (1974).

6. *Kelly v. Brewer,* 378 F.Supp. 447 (S.D. Iowa 1974); rev'd, in part, 525 F.2d 394 (8th Cir. 1975); *Clark v. Brewer,* No. 76-54-1 (S.D. Iowa).

7. *Bono v. Saxbe,* 450 F.Supp. at 945.

8. *Hewitt v. Helms,* — — — U.S. — — —, 74 L. Ed. 2d 673, 103 S.Ct. — — — (1983).

9. *Dudley v. Stewart,* No. 82-8428, 34 Cr. L. 2443 (CA 11 1984).

9. CONGRESSIONAL ACTIVITY AND DISCRETION IN THE CRIMINAL JUSTICE SYSTEM

1. Burton Atkins and Mark Pogrebin, "Introduction: Discretionary Decision Making in the Administration of Justice," in *The Invisible Justice System: Discretion and the Law*, ed. Burton Atkins and Mark Pogrebin (Cincinnati: Anderson, 1978), 1.

2. James L. LeGrande, *The Basic Process of Criminal Justice* (Beverly Hills, Calif.: Glencoe, 1973), 39.

3. President's Commission on Law Enforcement and Administration of Justice, Task Force Report: The Police (Washington, D.C.: Government Printing Office, 1967).

4. Norman Abrams, "Internal Policy: Guiding the Exercise of Prosecutorial Discretion," in Atkins and Pogrebin, *Invisible Justice System*, 231, 246–47.

5. National Advisory Commission on Criminal Justice Standards and Goals, *Courts* (Washington, D.C.: Government Printing Office, 1973), 46.

6. See, for example, Arthur Rosett, "Discretion, Severity and Legality in Criminal Justice," in Atkins and Pogrebin, *Invisible Justice System*, 24–33; Shari Diamond and Hans Zeisel, "Sentencing Councils: A Study of Sentence Disparity and Its Reduction," in Atkins and Pogrebin, 300–16; and Atkins and Pogrebin, 7.

7. Twentieth Century Fund Task Force on Criminal Sentencing *Fair and Certain Punishment* (New York: McGraw-Hill, 1976), 15–21.

8. Pierce O'Donnell, Michael J. Churgin, and Dennis E. Curtis, *Toward a Just and Effective Sentencing System* (New York: Praeger, 1977), 79.

9. David W. Neubauer, *America's Courts and the Criminal Justice System* (North Scituate, Mass.: Duxbury, 1979), 483.

10. Data was drawn from accounts of congressional activity included in the *Congressional Quarterly Almanacs*, 1960–1979, and the *Congressional Quarterly Weekly Reports*, 1980. In addition, House and Senate Judiciary Committee hearing reprints and reports were examined.

11. Senate Judiciary Committee, S. Rept. 372, June 28, 1967; quoted in *Congressional Quarterly Almanac*, 1967, 872.

12. In 1979 implementation of the new time limits set forth in the 1974 Speedy Trial Act were delayed until July 1, 1980.

13. David Mayhew, *Congress: The Electoral Connection* (New Haven: Yale Univ. Press, 1974), 5.

14. Morris Fiorina, *Congress: Keystone of the Washington Establishment* (New Haven: Yale Univ. Press, 1977), 41.

15. Albert Cover, "One Good Turn Deserves Another: The Advantage of Incumbency in Congressional Elections," *American Journal of Political Science*, 21(1977):539, and "Contacting Congressional Constituents: Some Patterns of Perquisite Use," *American Journal of Political Science* 24(1980):134.

16. Glenn Parker, "Sources of Change in Congressional District Attentiveness," *American Journal of Political Science* 24(1980):122-23.

17. This argument can also be found in Herbert B. Asher, "The Unintended Consequences of Legislative Professionalism," unpublished paper.

18. Lynette Perkins, "Influences of Member Goals on Their Committee Behavior: The U.S. House Judiciary Committee," *Legislative Studies Quarterly* 5(1980):376.

19. Morris Ogul, *Congress Oversees the Bureaucracy* (Pittsburgh: Univ. of Pittsburgh Press, 1976), 11.

20. Morris Ogul, "Legislative Oversight: Theory And Practice," in *The Congressional System: Notes and Readings,* ed. Rieselbach, 2d ed. (Belmont, Calif.: Duxbury, 1979), 347.

21. John Lees, "Legislatures and Oversight: A Review Article in a Neglected Area of Research," *Legislative Studies Quarterly* 2(1977):204–5.

10. MEDIATION AS AN ALTERNATIVE TO CIVIL RIGHTS LITIGATION

1. "Report and Recommendations on the Use of Arbitration," central legal staff, magistrates, and masters, presented to the Seventh Circuit's ad hoc committee to study the high cost of litigation, by the subcommittee on alternatives to the present federal court system, Nov. 1978.

2. "The Settlement Process," *Reports of the Conference for District Judges* (St. Paul: West, 1973), 252.

3. "Evaluation of the Pilot Project on Court-Referred Mediation" (Washington, D.C., Community Relations Service, Department of Justice, Feb. 1981).

11. DISCRETIONARY JUSTICE AT DOJ: IMPLEMENTING SECTION 5 OF THE VOTING RIGHTS ACT

1. Francis E. Rourke, *Bureaucracy, Politics, and Public Policy* (Boston: Little, Brown, 1969), 50.

2. Jeffrey L. Jowell, *Law and Bureaucracy* (Port Washington, New York: Dunellen Publishing, Inc., 1975), 156.

3. Kenneth Culp Davis, *Discretionary Justice: A Preliminary Inquiry* (Baton Rouge: Louisiana State Univ. Press, 1969).

4. Theodore J. Lowi, *The End of Liberalism: Ideology, Policy, and the Crisis of Public Authority* (New York: W. W. Norton and Co., Inc., 1969), 155; see also Chaps. 5 and 10.

5. *Allen v. State Board of Elections,* 393 U.S. 544 (1968).

6. *Perkins v. Matthews* 400 U.S. 379; 27 L. Ed 2d 476; 91 S.Ct. 431 (1970) at 391.

7. J. Stanley Pottinger, Assistant Attorney General, Civil Rights Division, U.S. Department of Justice, "Statement on Extension of the Voting Rights Act," Subcommittee on Civil Rights and Constitutional Rights, House Judiciary Committee, Mar. 5, 1975, 11.

8. David Hunter, *The Shameful Blight* (Washington, D.C.: Washington Research Project, 1972), 137–38.

9. *South Carolina v. Katzenbach,* 383 U.S. 301, 1966.

10. *Allen v. State Board of Elections,* 393 U.S. 547 (1969).

11. U.S. Comptroller General, *Voting Rights Act: Enforcement Needs Strengthening,* Washington, D.C.: General Accounting Office, Feb. 6, 1978, appendix IX.

12. The voting change preclearance process as outlined here has been reconstructed from interviews of officials in the Civil Rights Division and the Voting Section and from the information contained in the February 1978 GAO report on voting rights enforcement.

13. The problem of defining discrimination has provoked controversy within the Civil Rights Division that is manifested in two distinct perspectives. For more detail, see H. Ball, D. Krane, and T. Lauth, *Compromised Compliance: Implementation of the 1965 Voting Rights Act* (Westport, Conn.: Greenwood Press, 1982), Chap. 5.

14. U.S. Comptroller General, *Voting Rights Act:Enforcement Needs Strengthening,* Washington, D.C.: General Accounting Office, Feb. 6, 1978.

15. Interviews with attorneys in two jurisdictions that have had extensive involvement with DOJ lend credence to this contention. John Guyton, Kosciusko (Mississippi) city attorney, pointed out that the 1971 regulations were not clarified by DOJ until 1976, when litigation was entered into. He also noted that unlike the traditional voting rights litiga-tion, where lawyers had case law and precedent to work with, lawyers had little to work with when it came down to complying with Section 5 of the Voting Rights Act of 1965 and the 1971 regulations. Although John Ferguson, Fulton County (Atlanta) attorney agreed that it is unclear exactly what counts as evidence of nondiscrimination, he did indicate that he finds it important to rely upon what the courts are holding in related cases. Guyton interview, Kosciusko, Mississippi, March 6, 1978. Ferguson interview, Atlanta, Georgia, February 13, 1978.

16. Lowi, End of Liberalism, 300.

REFERENCES

BOOKS

Allen, Francis A. *The Borderland of Criminal Justice.* Chicago: Univ. of Chicago Press, 1964.

American Bar Association. *Standards Relating to Pleas of Guilty.* Chicago: American Bar Association, 1967.

American Friends Service Committee. *Struggle for Justice: A Report on Crime and Punishment in America.* New York: Hill and Wang, 1971.

Atkins, Burton, and Mark Pogrebin. *The Invisible Justice System: Discretion and the Law.* Cincinnati: Anderson, 1978.

Bazdekian, Ben, and Leon Dash. *The Shame of the Prison.* New York: Pocket Books, 1972.

Bent, Alan Edward. *The Politics of Law Enforcement.* Lexington, Mass.: D. C. Heath, 1974.

Bittner, Egon. *The Function of the Police in Modern Society.* Rockville, Md.: National Institute of Mental Health Center for Studies of Crime and Delinquency, 1970.

Blumberg, Abraham S. *Criminal Justice: Issues and Ironies.* New York: Franklin Watts, 1979.

Bond, James E. *Plea Bargaining and Guilty Pleas.* New York: Clark Boardman, 1975.

Braly, Malcolm. *On The Yard.* Greenwich, Conn.: Fawcett, 1972.

Brown, Michael K. *Working the Street: Police Discretion and the Dilemmas of Reform.* New York: Russell Sage, 1981.

Buckle, Suzann R. Thomas, and Leonard G. Buckle. *Bargaining for Justice: Case Disposition and Reform in the Criminal Courts.* New York: Praeger, 1977.

Carter, Lief H. *Administrative Law and Politics.* Boston: Little, Brown, 1983.

Casper, Jonathan D. *Criminal Courts: The Defendant's Perspective.* Washington, D.C.: Government Printing Office, 1978.

Chambliss, William, and Robert Seidman. *Law, Order, and Power.* Reading, Mass.: Addison-Wesley, 1971.

Chapman, Brian. *Police State.* New York: Praeger, 1970.

Chevigny, Paul. *Police Power.* New York: Pantheon Books, 1969.

Clemmer, Donald. *The Prison Community.* New York: Holt, Rinehart and Winston, 1958.

Cohen, Bernard, and Jan M. Chaikera. *Police Background Characteristics and Performance.* Santa Monica, Calif.: Rand Corp., 1972.

Cole, George F. *The American System of Criminal Justice.* North Scituate, Mass.: Duxbury, 1979.

Davis, Kenneth Culp. *Discretionary Justice: A Preliminary Inquiry.* Baton Rouge: Louisiana State Univ. Press, 1969.

———. *Police Discretion.* St. Paul, Minn.: West, 1975.

Dawson, Robert O. *Sentencing: The Decision as to Type, Length, and Conditions of Sentence.* Boston: Little, Brown, 1969.

Downie, Leonard. *Justice Denied.* New York: Praeger, 1971.

Dworkin, Ronald. *Taking Rights Seriously.* Cambridge, Mass.: Harvard Univ. Press, 1977.

Eisenstein, James, and Herbert Jacob. *Felony Justice.* Boston: Little, Brown, 1977.

Empey, Lamar T. *Alternatives to Incarceration.* Washington, D.C.: Government Printing Office, 1967.

Feeley, Malcolm M. *The Process is the Punishment: Handling Cases in Lower Criminal Court.* New York: Russell Sage, 1979.

Felkenes, George T. *The Criminal Justice System: Its Functions and Personnel.* Englewood Cliffs, N. J.: Prentice-Hall, 1973.

Fleming, Macklin. *The Price of Perfect Justice.* New York: Basic Books, 1974.

Fogel, David. *We Are the Living Proof: The Justice Model for Corrections.* Cincinnati: W. H. Anderson, 1975.

Frank, Benjamin, ed. *Contemporary Corrections.* Reston, Va.: Reston, 1973.

Frankel, Marvin. *Criminal Sentences: Law without Order.* New York: Hill and Wang, 1972.

Freed, Daniel, and Patricia Wald. *Bail in the United States: 1964.* Washington, D.C., Government Printing Office, 1964.

Gardiner, John A. *Traffic and the Police: Variations in Law Enforcement Policy.* Cambridge, Mass.: Harvard Univ. Press, 1969.

Gaylin, Willard. *Partial Justice.* New York: Alfred A. Knopf, 1974.

Glaser, Daniel. *The Effectiveness of a Prison and Parole System.* Indianapolis: Bobbs-Merrill, 1969.

Goldfarb, Ronald. *Ransom: A Critique of the Bail System.* New York: John Wiley, 1965.

Goldsmith, Jack, and Sharon S. Goldsmith. *The Police Community.* Pacific Palisades, Calif.: Palisades, 1974.

Goldstein, Abraham S. *The Passive Judiciary: Prosecutorial Discretion and the Guilty Plea.* Baton Rouge: Louisiana State Univ. Press, 1981.

Goldstein, Herman. *Policing a Free Society.* Cambridge, Mass.: Ballinger, 1977.

Goulden, Joseph C. *The Benchwarmers: The Private World of the Powerful Federal Judges.* New York: Ballantine, 1974.

Green, Edward. *Judicial Attitudes in Sentencing.* New York: St. Martin's, 1961.

Greenberg, Douglas. *Crime and Law Enforcement in the Colony of New York, 1691–1776.* Ithaca, N.Y.: Cornell Univ. Press, 1976.

Grosman, Brian A. *The Prosecutor: A Inquiry into the Exercise of Discretion.* Toronto: Univ. of Toronto Press, 1969.

Harris, Richard. *Justice: The Crisis of Law, Order and Freedom in America.* New York: E. P. Dutton, 1970.

Heumann, Milton. *Plea Bargaining: The Experiences of Prosecutors, Judges, and Defense Attorneys.* Chicago: Univ. of Chicago Press, 1977.

Hogarth, John. *Sentencing as a Human Process.* Toronto: Univ. of Toronto Press, 1971.

Jacoby, Joan. *The American Prosecutor: A Search for Identity.* Lexington, Mass.: Lexington Books, D. C. Heath, 1980.

Kalmanoff, Alan. *Criminal Justice: Enforcement and Administration.* Boston: Little, Brown, 1976.

Katz, Lewis R. *The Justice Imperative.* Cincinnati: Anderson, 1980.

Klein, John F. *Let's Make a Deal.* Lexington, Mass.: Lexington Books, 1976.

LaFave, Wayne R. *Arrest: The Decision to Take a Suspect into Custody.* Boston: Little, Brown, 1965.

――――. *Modern Criminal Law.* St. Paul, Minn.: West, 1978.

LeGrande, James L. *The Basic Process of Criminal Justice.* Beverly Hills, Calif.: Glencoe, 1973.

Levin, Martin A. *Urban Politics and Criminal Courts.* Chicago: Univ. of Chicago Press, 1977.

Littrell, W. Boyd. *Bureaucratic Justice.* Beverly Hills, Calif.: Sage, 1979.

Louthan, William C. *The Politics of Justice.* Port Washington, N.Y.: Kennikat, 1979.

Manning, Peter K. *Police Work.* Cambridge, Mass.: MIT Press, 1977.

Mather, Lynn. *Plea Bargaining or Trial?* Lexington, Mass.: D. C. Heath, 1979.

Miller, Frank W. *Prosecution: The Decision to Charge a Suspect with a Crime.* Boston: Little, Brown, 1969.

Mitford, Jessica. *Kind and Usual Punishment.* New York: Alfred A. Knopf, 1973.

Moley, Raymond. *Politics and Criminal Prosecutions.* New York: Minton, Balch, 1929.

Morris, Norval. *The Future of Imprisonment.* Chicago: Univ. of Chicago Press, 1974.

Muir, William K. *Police: Streetcorner Politicians.* Chicago: Univ. of Chicago Press, 1977.

Nagel, Stuart S., and Mariann Neff. *The Legal Process: Modeling the System.* Beverly Hills, Calif.: Sage, 1977.

National Center for State Courts. *An Evaluation of Policy Related Research on the Effectiveness of Pretrial Release Programs.* Denver: National Center for State Courts, 1975.

Neubauer, David W. *Criminal Justice in Middle America.* Morristown, N.J.: General Learning, 1974.

———. *America's Courts and the Criminal Justice System.* North Scituate, Mass.: Duxbury, 1979.

Newman, Donald J. *Conviction: The Determining of Guilt or Innocence without Trial.* Boston: Little, Brown, 1966.

Niederhoffer, Arthur. *Behind the Shield: The Police in Urban Society.* Garden City, N.J.: Anchor Books, 1969.

O'Donnell, Pierce, Michael J. Churgin, and Dennis E. Curtis. *Toward a Just and Effective Sentencing System.* New York: Praeger, 1977.

Ohein, Lloyd E. *Prisoners in America.* Englewood Cliffs, N.J.: Prentice-Hall, 1973.

Orland, Leonard. *Prisons: Houses of Darkness.* New York: Free Press, 1975.

Packer, Herbert L. *The Limits of the Criminal Sanction.* Stanford, Calif.: Stanford Univ. Press, 1968.

Pound, Roscoe. *Criminal Justice in America.* New York: Holt, 1930.

Quinney, Richard, ed. *Criminal Justice in America: A Critical Understanding.* Boston: Little, Brown, 1974.

Rawls, John. *A Theory of Justice.* Cambridge, Mass.: Harvard Univ. Press, Belknap Press, 1971.

Rosett, Arthur, and Donald R. Cressey. *Justice by Consent.* New York: J. B. Lippincott, 1976.

Rudovsky, David. *The Rights of Prisoners: The Basic ACLU Guide to a Prisoner's Rights.* New York: Avon, 1973.

Sartori, Giovanni. *Democratic Theory.* New York: Frederick A. Praeger, 1965.

Skolnick, Jerome H. *Justice without Trial: Law Enforcement in a Democratic Society.* New York: John Wiley, 1977.

Stanley, David. *Prisoners Among Us.* Washington, D.C.: The Brookings Institute, 1976.

Sutton, Paul L. *Federal Sentencing Patterns: A Study of Geographical Variations.* Albany, N.Y.: Criminal Justice Research Center, 1978.

———. *Variations in Federal Criminal Sentences: A Statistical Assessment at the National Level.* Albany, N.Y.: Criminal Justice Research Center, 1979.

Sykes, Gresham M. *The Society of Captives.* New York: Atheneum, 1965.

Thomas, Wayne H., Jr. *Bail Reform in America.* Berkeley, Calif.: Univ. of California Press, 1976.

———. *Pretrial Release Programs.* Washington, D.C.: National Institute of Law Enforcement and Criminal Justice, 1977.

Turk, Austin. *Criminality and the Legal Order.* Chicago: Rand McNally, 1969.

Twentieth-Century Fund. *Fair and Certain Punishment: Report of the Twentieth-Century Fund Task Force on Criminal Sentencing.* New York: McGraw-Hill, 1976.

U.S. Commission on Civil Rights. *Who Is Guarding the Guardians? A Report on Police Practices.* Washington, D.C.: Government Printing Office, 1981.

U.S. National Advisory Commission on Criminal Justice Standards and Goals: Courts. Washington, D.C.: Government Printing Office, 1973.

Utz, Pamela. *Settling the Facts: Discretion and Negotiation in Criminal Court.* Lexington, Mass.: D. C. Heath, 1978.

Vera Institute of Justice. *Programs in Criminal Justice Reform: Ten Year Report, 1961–1971.* New York: Vera Institute, 1972.
_____. *Felony Arrests: Their Prosecution and Disposition in New York City's Courts.* New York: Vera Institute, 1977.
Vollmer, August. *The Police in Modern Society.* Berkeley, Calif.: Univ. of California Press, 1936.
Von Hirsh, A., and K. J. Hanrahan. *Abolish Parole?* Washington, D.C.: Law Enforcement Assistance Administration, 1978.
Walker, Samuel. *Popular Justice: A History of American Criminal Justice.* New York: Oxford Univ. Press, 1980.
Wice, Paul B. *Freedom for Sale: A National Study of Pretrial Release.* Lexington, Mass.: Lexington Books, 1974.
Wilson, James Q. *Varieties of Police Behavior.* Cambridge, Mass.: Harvard Univ. Press, 1968.
Wolin, Sheldon. *Politics and Vision.* Boston: Little, Brown, 1960.
Wood, Gordon S. *The Creation of the American Republic: 1776–1787.* Chapel Hill: Univ. of North Carolina Press, 1969.

ARTICLES

Abrams, Norman. "Prosecutorial Discretion." *UCLA Law Review* 19(1971):1–58.
Alper, Benedict S., and Joseph W. Weise. "The Mandatory Sentence: Recipe for Retribution." *Federal Probation* 41(1977):15–20.
Alschuler, Albert W. "The Prosecutor's Role in Plea Bargaining." *University of Chicago Law Review* 36(1968):50–112.
_____. "The Trial Judge's Role in Plea Bargaining." *Columbia Law Review* 86(1976):1064–1154.
_____. "The Defense Attorney's Role in Plea Bargaining." *Yale Law Journal* 84(1978):1288–1320.
_____. "Plea Bargaining and its History." *Law and Society Review* 13(1979):211–45.
Ares, Charles, Anne Rankin, and Herbert Sturz. "The Manhattan Bail Project: An Interim Report on the Use of Pre-trial Parole." *New York University Law Review* 38(1963):82–84.
Barrett, Edward L. "Police Practices and the Law: From Arrest to Release or Charge." *California Law Review* 50(1962):11–55.
Battle, Jackson B. "In Search of the Adversary System: The Cooperative Practices of Private Criminal Defense Attorneys." *University of Texas Law Review* 50(1971):66–88.
Blumberg, Abraham. "The Practice of Law as a Confidence Game." *Law and Society Review* 1(1967):11–39.
Brereton, David, and Jonathan D. Casper. "Does it Pay to Plead Guilty? Differential Sentencing and the Functioning of Criminal Courts." *Law and Society Review* 16(1981–82):45–70.
Carroll, John S., Richard L. Wiener, Dan Coates, Jolene Galegher, and James J. Alibrio. "Evaluation, Diagnosis, and Prediction in Parole Decision Making." *Law and Society Review* 17(1982):199–228.
Carter, Lief H. "Flexibility and Uniformity in Criminal Justice." *Policy Studies Journal.* 3(1974):18–25.
Carter, Robert M., and Leslie T. Wilkins. "Some Factors in Sentencing Policy." *Journal of Criminal Law, Criminology and Police Science* 58(1967):503–14.
Cole, George F. "The Decision to Prosecute." *Law and Society Review* 4(Feb. 1970):313–43.
Cole, George F., and Charles H. Logan. "Parole: The Consumer's Perspective." *Criminal Justice Review* 1(1977):32–55.
Czajkoski, Eugene. "Exposing the Quasi-Judicial Role of the Probation Officer." *Federal Probation* 37(1973):9–13.

Daig, Jameson W. "Juvenile Justice: Discretionary Power and the Control of Youth." *Policy Studies Journal* 3(1974):66–74.

David, Lane. "The Cost of Realism: Contemporary Restatements of Democracy." *Western Political Quarterly* 17(Mar. 1964):37–46.

D'Esposito, Julian C., Jr. "Sentencing Disparity: Causes and Cures." *Journal of Criminal Law, Criminology and Policy Science* 60(1969):183–205.

Dill, Forest. "Discretion, Exchange and Social Control: Bail Bondsmen in Criminal Courts." *Law and Society Review* 9(1975):639–74.

Fairchild, Erika S. "New Perspectives on Corrections Policy." *Policy Studies Journal* 3(1974):74–82.

Feeley, Malcolm M. "Perspectives on Plea Bargaining." *Law and Society Review* 13(1979):199–209.

Felkenes, George T. "The Prosecutor: A Look at Reality." *Southwestern University Law Review* 7(1975):98–123.

Flemming, Roy B., C. W. Kohfeld, and Thomas M. Uhlman. "The Limits of Bail Reform: A Quasi-Experimental Analysis." *Law and Society Review* 14(1980):947–76.

Friedman, Lawrence M. "Plea Bargaining in Historical Perspective." *Law and Society Review* 13(1979):247–59.

Goldman, Sheldon. "In Defense of Justice: Some Thoughts on Reading Professor Mendelson's 'Mr. Justice Douglas and Government by the Judiciary.' " *Journal of Politics* 1(Feb. 1977):152.

Goldstein, Herman. "Police Discretion: The Ideal Versus the Real." *Public Administration Review* 23(1963):140–48.

Goldstein, Joseph. "Police Discretion Not to Invoke the Criminal Process: Low-Visibility Decisions in the Administration of Justice." *Yale Law Journal* 69(1960):543–89.

Haller, Mark H. "Plea Bargaining: The Nineteenth-Century Context." *Law and Society Review* 13(1979):273–79.

Hier, A. P. "Curbing Abuse in the Decision to Grant or Deny Parole." *Harvard Civil Rights and Civil Liberties Law Review* 8(1973):419–68.

Holden, Pauline. "Impact of Procedural Modifications on Evaluations of Plea Bargaining." *Law and Society Review* 15(1980–1981):267–91.

Johnson, James N. "The Influence of Politics Upon the Office of the American Prosecutor." *American Journal of Criminal Law* 2(1973):187–215.

Joseph, Roger P. "Reviewability of Prosecutorial Discretion: Failure to Prosecute." *Columbia Law Review* 75(1975):130–61.

Kadish, Sanford H. "Legal Norm and Discretion in the Policy and Sentencing Process." *Harvard Law Review* 74(1962):904–31.

Kann, Mark E. "Challenging Lockean Liberalism in America: The Case of Debs and Hilquit." *Political Theory* 8, no. 2(May 1980):203–22.

Kaplan, John. "The Prosecutorial Discretion — A Comment." *Northwestern Law Review* 60(1965):176–93.

Kruttschnitt, Candace. "Social Status and Sentences of Female Offenders." *Law and Society Review* 15(1980–1981):247–65.

LaFave, Wayne R. "The Prosecutor's Discretion in the United States." *American Journal of Comparative Law* 18(1970):532–48.

Langbein, John H. "Understanding the Short History of Plea Bargaining." *Law and Society Review* 13(1979):261–72.

Louthan, William C. "Relationships Among Police, Court, and Correctional Agencies." *Policy Studies Journal* 3(Autumn 1974):30–37.

———. "Paradigms of Police Community: A New Critique of Legal Order." *Public Administration Review* 3(1975).

Mashaw, Jerry L. "Conflict and Compromise Among Models of Administrative Justice." *Duke Law Journal* (1981):181–214.

McCleary, Richard. "How Structural Variables Constrain the Parole Officer's Use of Discretionary Powers." *Social Problems* 23(1975):209–25.

Mulkey, Michael A. "The Role of Prosecution and Defense in Plea Bargaining." *Policy Studies Journal* 3(1974):54–60.

Parnas, Raymond I. "Police Discretion and Diversion of Incidents of Intra-Family Violence." *Law and Contemporary Problems* 36(1971):539–65.

Petersen, David M., and Paul C. Friday. "Early Release from Incarceration." *Journal of Criminal Law and Criminology* 66(1975):79–87.

Philips, Michael. "The Question of Voluntariness in the Plea Bargaining Controversy: A Philosophical Perspective." *Law and Society Review* 16(1981–1982):207–24.

Pierce, Lawrence W. "Rehabilitation in Corrections: A Reassessment." *Federal Probation* 68(1974):15–30.

Poole, Eric D., and Robert M. Regoli. "Race, Institutional Rule Breaking, and Disciplinary Response: A Study of Discretionary Decision Making in Prison." *Law and Society Review* 14(1980):931–46.

Reiss, Albert J., Jr. "Discretionary Justice in the United States." *International Journal of Criminology and Penology* 2(1974):181–205.

Rhodes, Robert P. "Political Theory, Policy Analysis, and the Insoluble Problems of Criminal Justice." *Policy Studies Journal* 3(1974):83–89.

Ruckelman, Leonard. "Police Policy." *Policy Studies Journal* 3(1974):48–53.

Ryan, John Paul. "Adjudication and Sentencing in a Misdemeanor Court: The Outcome is the Punishment." *Law and Society Review* 15(1980–1981):79–108.

Spohn, Cassia, John Gruhl, and Susan Welch. "The Effect of Race on Sentencing: A Re-Examination of an Unsettled Question." *Law and Society Review* 16(1981–1982):71–88.

Stanko, Elizabeth Anne. "The Impact of Victim Assessment on Prosecutors' Screening Decisions: The Case of the New York County District Attorney's Office." *Law and Society Review* 16(1981–1982):225–39.

Uviller, H. Richard. "The Virtuous Prosecutor in Quest of an Ethical Standard: Guidance from the ABA." *Michigan Law Review* 71(1973):1145–68.

Wilson, James Q. "The Police and Their Problems: A Theory." *Public Policy* 12(1963):189–216.

Yale Law Journal, Note. "Bargaining in Correctional Institutions: Restructuring the Relation Between the Inmate and Prison Authority." *Yale Law Journal* 81(1972):726–40.

INDEX

Abrams, Norman, *44n. 1,* 52
Accountability: and democracy, 3
Ackerman, Judge J. Waldo, 93
Acton, Lord, 4, 5
Administrative discretion, 103-4
Administrative Solid Lockup (ASL): in Iowa, 72-80
Air traffic controllers strike, 1981, 5-6
Allen v. State Board of Elections, 105, 107
American Bar Foundation, 14
American Law Institute, 23
The American Prosecutor, 25
Aristotle, 9, 11
Arizona, 23-24
Arkansas, 22, 23
Arnold, Thurman, 45
Arzt, Gunther, 49
Augustine, Isreal M. Jr., 57-59
Autonomy: and discretion, x

Bail: decison making, Hamilton County, Ohio, 36-43; and judges, 82; in Ohio, 31; reform, 32-33; reform in Ohio, 33-43
Bail Reform Act, 83-84
Benn, S. I., 10
Berry, Brian, 8
Bittner, Egon, 66
Blizzard, Janet, 112
Brewer, Lou V., 74, 76
Brooklyn, N.Y. District Attorney's Office, 47
Brown v. Board of Education, 6
Bua, Judge Nicholas J., 93
Bureaucracy: and arbitrary decisions, 15-16

Cairo, Illinois: voting rights case, 95-96
California: and parole, 63

Celler, Emanuel, 87
Chastain v. the Civil Service Board of Orlando, 29
Chicago Overall Economic Development Plan, 94, 96
Chicago Park District, 94
Cincinnati, 33
Citation system, 22-23
City of St. Petersburg v. Reed, 29
Civiletti, Attorney General Benjamin R., 97
Civilian review boards: and police, 27
Civil rights: groups, 106-7; and mediation, 90-101; Reagan administration policy, 6-7; and 7th federal circuit, 92-101
Civil Rights Act, 1964: Title X, 90; Title II, 91
Civil Rights Division: Nixon reorganization, 105-6; and Section 5, Voting Rights Act, 104-5; and submission regulations (28 CFR Part 51), 107-8; Voting Section, 102
Clark, Edward, 74, 78
Clark v. Brewer, 72, 74, 77, 78, 79-80
Close Management (CM), 77-80
Colorado, 47
Community involvement: and CRS, 94
Community Relations Service (CRS), 90-101; and community involvement, 94; and corrections, 92-93; and employment, 93; and housing, 93-94; mediation results, 94-101; and voting rights, 93
Congress: attempts at limiting discretion, 83-86; and discretion, 81-89; failure to limit discretion, 86-89; and federal parole procedures, 85; and reelection, 86-88; and reform of federal code, 84-85
Cook County Jail: segregation case, 96-97
Corrections: and CRS, 92-93
Cover, Albert, 87
Cramton, Roger G.: and judicial review, 52
Creativity: and discretion, 50
Criminal Code Reform Act, 84